THE
FULL TANK LIFE

THE
FULL TANK LIFE

FUEL YOUR DREAMS,
IGNITE YOUR DESTINY

BEN
TANKARD

New York   Nashville

FaithWords
Hachette Book Group
1290 Avenue of the Americas
New York, NY 10104
faithwords.com
twitter.com/faithwords

First Edition: August 2016

FaithWords is a division of Hachette Book Group, Inc.
The FaithWords name and logo are trademarks of Hachette Book Group, Inc.

The publisher is not responsible for websites (or their content) that are not owned by the publisher.

The Hachette Speakers Bureau provides a wide range of authors for speaking events. To find out more, go to www.hachettespeakersbureau.com or call (866) 376-6591.

Unless otherwise noted, all Scripture quotations are taken from The Holy Bible, New International Version (NIV). Copyright © 1973, 1978, 1984, 2011 by Biblica, Inc. Used by permission of Zondervan. All rights reserved worldwide. (www.zondervan.com).

Scripture quotations marked NKJV are taken from the New King James Version. Copyright © 1982 by Thomas Nelson, Inc. Used by permission. All rights reserved. Scripture quotations marked CEV are taken from the Contemporary English Version. Copyright © 1995 by the American Bible Society. Used by permission. Scripture quotations marked TLB are taken from The Living Bible. Copyright © 1971. Used by permission of Tyndale House Publishers, Inc., Carol Stream, Illinois 60188. All rights reserved. Scripture quotations marked KJV are taken from the King James Version of the Bible. Scripture quotations marked ESV are taken from the ESV® Bible (The Holy Bible, English Standard Version®) copyright © 2001 by Crossway, a publishing ministry of Good News Publishers. ESV® Text Edition: 2011. Scripture quotations marked MSG are taken from The Message. Copyright © 1993, 1994, 1995, 1996, 2000, 2001, 2002. Used by permission of NavPress Publishing Group. Scripture quotations marked NASB are taken from the NEW AMERICAN STANDARD BIBLE®, Copyright © 1960,1962,1963,1968,1971,1972,1973,1975,1977,1995 by The Lockman Foundation. Used by permission. Scripture quotations marked NLT are taken from the Holy Bible, New Living Translation, copyright © 1996, 2004, 2015 by Tyndale House Foundation. Used by permission of Tyndale House Publishers Inc., Carol Stream, Illinois 60188. All rights reserved.

Library of Congress Cataloging-in-Publication Data has been applied for.

ISBNs: 978-1-4555-3829-4 (hardcover), 978-1-4555-3830-0 (ebook)

Printed in the United States of America

RRD-C

10 9 8 7 6 5 4 3 2 1

To Jewel, my lovely wife and best friend.

When I first met you I said to myself, "The Lord is my shepherd; I see what I want!" I never dreamed life with you would be so glorious. You are my love, my biggest fan and cheerleader, and my most trusted adviser. You are so pretty, sweet, and loving that every day with you is like celebrating our anniversary.

To our children, Marcus, Brooklyn, Britney, Benji, and Cyrene; as well as my two daughters-in-law, Tish and Shanira; three grandkids, Diamond, Micah, and Billie (Benja-Mina); and one grandpuppy, Buddy. You all inspire me to be the man God intended me to be. I am honored to be your "paw-paw," and I am so thankful for our blended family and legacy of love.

CONTENTS

DESTINY—Accelerating toward Greatness

A map is only good when you know your starting point. Tell the truth about where you are without diminishing where you want to be.

Have you ever driven a car with the low-fuel light on? What a nervous ride! When you know that at any time the car could run out of fuel and force you to walk, it makes for a very uncomfortable trip. Most of us would rather have a full tank of gas even if our journey is not that long. There is a special confidence that comes from knowing you have more than enough fuel for your drive. Your fuel level becomes even more important when flying a plane (there are no gas stations in the sky) and absolutely critical when applied to your life.

Do you have a Full Tank Life?

There are countless books written on topics such as happiness, success, and personal fulfillment. The people writing these books are super smart and many have more degrees than a thermometer behind their name! Yet the secret to enjoying the uniqueness of who you are, where you are, and where you're going seems to elude most people. Obviously, there's no one-size-fits-all formula with three easy steps. We each have a variety of gifts and talents, dreams and aspirations, as well as experiences and opportunities that we bring to life each day. From my experience, the secret to success is simply getting all these items in alignment. Which I know firsthand is not always easy—especially when life seems to place obstacles in your path on a daily basis.

In fact, roughly eight out of ten people in our country are not content with their present lives. In other words, only about 20 percent of the population would say they're enjoying their lives to the fullest, living what I like to call the Full Tank Life, which is basically just doing what you were born to do. The happiest people in the world seem to be those who have tapped into their God-given talents and inner passions. They've grown from their past, they're engaged with their present, and they're excited about their future. If people notice how much I enjoy my life right now, it's because I'm happier than I've ever been, pursuing the goals that express who I am at the core of my being. I'm loving my wife and leading our family, making and producing music, pastoring and mentoring our church, speaking and acting, piloting my plane, and doing a host of other activities that bring me joy because they're vital to who I am, to the way God made me.

Another big part of what brings me joy is inspiring others to find their purpose and live their best Full Tank Life. And that's what this book is all about. Nothing would make me happier than to sit down and have a conversation with you about who you are and what you want your life to be about. But since we may not get that opportunity face-to-face, I hope that we can begin a different kind of conversation through these pages. Although we may be separated by distance, our hearts will be united in the pursuit of our shared goal: filling your life's tank and igniting your dreams. My job is to show you how to uncover those suppressed gifts and to set goals to experience a constant path of growth and fulfillment for the rest of your life. I'm convinced that once you know your assignment in life, it will strengthen and lengthen every area of your life.

The good news is that the keys to your Full Tank Life are already in front of you. Yes, all the answers you're looking for have already been found. There are no secrets to your success (just because you don't know something doesn't mean it's a secret!). You simply haven't discovered how to activate and implement what you already know about yourself. Information is like a radio station broadcast. The music is in the air all the time, but you won't be able to hear it until you tune in your radio receiver. If you cut the radio off, the music is still playing; you just don't hear it. But just because you're not tuned in to a certain channel of information doesn't mean it's a secret. This data was there all along; you just were not tuned in.

So it's time to awaken the sleeping giant inside you, the one named Destiny. "Hello, this is Ben Tankard down at the front desk in the lobby of your dreams. My friend, this *is* your wake-up call!" It's time to tune in, tank up, and take off!

And before you make excuses or dismiss me as just another

pep-talk motivator, let me share a few things about what happened when I woke up and began living out my Full Tank Life. You see, my Destiny has wings. It has taken me to every corner of the globe. I have been able to see the world, pilot my own airplanes to many of these locations, dine in fine restaurants, meet extraordinary people, perform concerts with people I admired for years who are now my friends, smooth jazz and gospel greats like Yolanda Adams, Kirk Whalum, Jonathan Butler, Kirk Franklin and CeCe Winans, and the late, great Wayman Tisdale.

My Full Tank Life has brought me into fellowship and friendship with great men and women, presidents of state, awesome speakers, pastors, and mentors like Creflo Dollar, Joel Osteen, and Bishop T. D. Jakes. I have been blessed to speak to crowds of over twenty thousand people. Living with a Full Tank has opened doors for me to live the good life, call a modern palace my home, relax in exotic locales, and have my own reality show on TV. But the biggest blessing of all is I get to help people. When you tap into your true calling in life, then you will automatically be in the business of helping people. Everyone has a certain place to fit in on earth. You are a piece of the ultimate puzzle. You have a part to play in other people's Destiny, and you can only do it by walking in yours.

There are many books out there on life fulfillment, but I sincerely believe what I have to share will reach a place in your heart that will excite you and motivate you toward change. Believe me, I do not claim to know everything (in fact, I am a college dropout); however, what I've learned I will gladly share with you.

If you're reading these words right now, then you've already tapped into something it takes to awaken your Destiny—desire.

You obviously want more from life than you've got right now or you wouldn't have read this far!

So let me make a few recommendations about how you can best use this book. First, you do *not* have to read the chapters in sequential order. I've organized what I know about the Full Tank Life around seven areas based on what I consider the key parts of your Destiny. Each chapter of the book explores one of these seven—dreams, environment, subconscious, time, inspiration, network, and you—which together form your Destiny. Once aligned, these will help you tap into your life purpose, fill your motivational tank, and ignite the power to be all that you are meant to be.

Within each chapter you will find some homework assignments to help you put in practice what we've been exploring in that particular area. You will also discover some blank lines at the end of each chapter called "Your DESTINY Diary" where you can respond to my final questions designed to help you both summarize and personalize what you've just learned. In addition, you will notice quotations from some of my favorite mentors, teachers, and role models, along with some of my own, all identified as a "BENspiration" to fill your mental, emotional, and spiritual tanks.

I believe that in order for any "self-help" to have a lasting impact on you it must be read at least three times. In fact, I've heard it said that one has to hear a message seven times before one decides to act on it. With the power of repetition in mind, I have restated many of my key points across all chapters and have tried to help you see my big ideas from multiple angles.

So I encourage you to read this book more than once, to skip around in it based on what jumps out at you, to mark up favorite chapters and highlight key areas. So grab your yellow highlighter and a pen or pencil (or your phone or tablet), and let's dig in and create a flight plan for the journey of ascension on which you're about to embark. It's time for you to begin pouring into your Full Tank Life!

BENspiration

Even if you are on the right road, if you don't move you will be run over! Let's go!

THE
FULL TANK LIFE

CHAPTER 1

Flying on the Wings of DESTINY

Getting Ready for Takeoff

You're where you're supposed to be—but not where you're going.

I don't get it.

Every year I witness family, friends, colleagues, and fans getting caught in the New Year's frenzy of setting new goals and resolutions. Everyone is talking about what's coming *next*, and the thought of these dreams coming true creates its own energy and excitement. Many of these goals are related to their physical health, their weight, and their lifestyle habits.

During those first days of January each year, the number of new memberships at gyms and health clubs skyrocket as people make the decision that *this* will be the year their resolutions finally endure and produce the intended fruit of thinner, leaner bodies. This will be the year when they finally dig deep and make it happen. This will be the year when they change old habits, commit to new ones, and discover something within themselves that they know is there but hasn't come out yet. This will be the year when they fulfill their dormant potential and transform their opportunity to change into who they want to be, who they believe they're meant to be.

Their hopeful exhilaration is almost like having your name called on *The Price Is Right* game show to "come on down!" I'm always amazed at the prospective contestant whose name gets called. They get so excited, jumping and screaming and rushing down front—and they haven't even won anything yet! They've only won the *opportunity* to win something. But simply the *thought* of winning, the possibility in itself, gets them into a frenzy, and nothing can stop them from running to the front of the auditorium.

But what's so special about January 1? Does something change in the atmosphere that makes it easier to exercise and lose weight? Do old habits suddenly peel away as easily as the December page from last year's calendar? Of course not!

So what if you made a point on a daily basis—starting right now, right here, wherever you are—to create the expectation for positive change to begin in your life? What would happen if you knew nothing could stop you from succeeding and bringing your dreams to life? What would it feel like to know you absolutely could not fail? For your life to take flight in thrilling ways you can barely imagine?

Can you feel it?

God has made you the CEO of your own life. He has created you with unique gifts that no one who has ever lived throughout history has had. Your Creator has instilled within your DNA the very essence of His own divine image and holy imagination.

You're not God—neither am I, thankfully—but we're all created by the Master Artist and carry within us His divine design.

Just consider all the incredible beauty of God's creation. A desert sunset sinking into its gold-orange-pink horizon. The lush Amazon jungle teeming with a symphony of sounds and colors. The shape of an elephant's trunk. The smell of roses wafting from a bride's bouquet. The architectural marvel of form and function that is the human body. All of these gifts and countless others stagger our senses with their beauty and complexity. And all of them originated from the divine imagination of God—*just like you!*

You don't have to wait until January to start your new life. You don't have to wait until you have more money. You don't have to wait until you finish your degree, get married, start a family, or launch a website. You don't have to know all the answers or even all the questions.

You only have to make one decision. A choice to stop settling for life on the ground when you know you were meant to fly. A choice to seize the opportunity God has placed before you.

The choice to live a Full Tank Life.

Getting Your Dreams Off the Ground

When I decided to pursue my dream of becoming a pilot, I realized that it would mean overcoming some of my fears. It would mean stretching outside my comfort zone and pushing myself beyond my normal limits. And I learned early in my training that in order to have a smooth takeoff, you have to do a lot of preparation on the ground. In order to ever get off the ground, you have to know your present location as well as where you're going.

Launching your dreams toward your Destiny requires similar ground preparation before you soar to new heights. We'll unpack all the facets of a Full Tank Life throughout the rest of the book, but before we begin, you have to want to begin. You have to want to make a change and to start *right now.* Not tomorrow, not next week, not after the holidays or when you get that big promotion. As my friend Joel Osteen is so fond of saying, "Your time is now!"

You picked up this book for a reason. Maybe you're a fan of my gospel jazz music. Or maybe you love watching the antics of my crazy family on *Thicker Than Water: The Tankards* on Bravo. Or maybe you've never heard of Ben Tankard but you're intrigued by the title, curious about what it takes to have a Full Tank after running on empty for so long.

Whatever the reason, it's no accident my book is in your hands.

It's time to go after your dreams as if your life depends on it. Why? Because it does!

So many people feel trapped in their lives. They had big dreams when they were children, but as they got older and experienced the ways the world works, their dreams started to evaporate. By the time they were teenagers, young adults making plans for their future, they began to bump against limitations.

Can you relate? Maybe you didn't get to go to the college you wanted because your family couldn't afford it. Maybe you couldn't afford to go to college at all. Or maybe an unplanned pregnancy rushed you into parenthood before you were able to grow your dreams. It could be taking care of your parents or another loved one that's made it necessary for you to hit the pause button on your future. You might have an illness or injury that's been chronic and debilitating, derailing your dreams. Perhaps you feel trapped in a dead-end job.

Believe me, I understand all of those circumstances—because I've lived through them! I've been a garbage collector, a chicken farmer, and a college dropout. I've gone through detours, divorces, depression, and disappointments. But through them all, the spark of my dreams has never been quenched. Oh, I tried sometimes to snuff that tiny flame. Because when you can't see a way to move forward, when you feel stuck and trapped by your circumstances, then it can be too painful to think about your dreams. Thoughts of them mock you and make you feel foolish for ever hoping, let alone trying to be more than you are at the moment.

But your story is not over. Your game is still in play. The last chapter has not been written.

Even with all of life's limitations, setbacks, responsibilities, and obligations, it's never too late for you to still experience the Full Tank Life. Your dreams are the key to unlocking that feeling of being trapped by your past choices or your responsibilities to others. When you commit to making your dreams a reality, then you will be surprised how quickly you will feel liberated and fulfilled. When you're riding with a Full Tank, the journey is just as joyful as the destination!

And it all starts with resuscitating your dreams. Like a lifeguard dragging a drowning swimmer to shore and performing CPR to revive them, you must find the spark of life still burning within. You must dare to believe and to step out in faith. You must bring your hope back to life.

BENspiration

"There are two primary choices in life: to accept conditions as they exist, or accept the responsibility for changing them."

—*Denis Waitley*

Hope Floats

If you feel silly resurrecting your dreams because they seem grandiose and farfetched, then you're probably on the right track. Because God wants your dreams so big and so impossible that you absolutely have to live by faith. He wants you taking risks and depending on Him in order to accomplish the dreams He's planted within you, the impossible kind of goals that you could never achieve in your own power. In fact, the Bible tells us, "And without faith it is impossible to please God, because anyone who comes to him must believe that he exists and that he rewards those who earnestly seek him" (Heb. 11:6).

One of the most dramatic stories of being faithful to an impossible dream comes from a guy who ended up being the world's first sailor. Actually, he was the world's first boat builder and zookeeper as well. Noah was an ordinary person called to do extraordinary things. We're told he "found favor" with the Lord at a time when hardly anyone else honored God (Gen. 6:8).

He lived in times every bit as turbulent as ours. Almost

everyone on earth had forsaken God and started to live like there was no tomorrow—partying, pillaging, and polluting, doing whatever they wanted or felt like doing. They mocked the few people who still had faith in God, like Noah's family, and felt like they were on top of the world. But that all changed when the rain began to fall.

You see, God became sick and tired of the way men and women—His own creation—had abused the gift of free will by abandoning Him and His ways. People were so violent, greedy, lustful, and selfish that God did something He had never done before, something so extreme that He promised never to do it again: hit the reset button on the human race and start all over again. Here's how it's described in Genesis:

> The LORD saw how great the wickedness of the human race had become on the earth, and that every inclination of the thoughts of the human heart was only evil all the time. The LORD regretted that he had made human beings on the earth, and his heart was deeply troubled. So the LORD said, "I will wipe from the face of the earth the human race I have created—and with them the animals, the birds and the creatures that move along the ground—for I regret that I have made them." But Noah found favor in the eyes of the LORD.
>
> *Genesis 6:5–8*

The favor Noah found in God's eyes resulted in the building of the ark. And the Lord was very specific about how Noah was to build it, outfit it, and stock it with a pair of every kind of animal in existence (see Gen. 6:14–21). The level of detail in God's instructions to His chosen dreamer rival those from a gourmet chef cooking a seven-course meal! I tease my wife Jewel about never cooking, and if she had to follow instructions like this, then I'd be a starving man!

But your dreams are in the details. Are we told whether Noah had any carpentry skills or construction expertise? No, we're not, because when God gives you a dream—in Noah's case, a dream that was literally going to save his life and the lives of his family, not to mention the human race—it doesn't matter. God will provide everything you need and teach you on the fly how to be ready, resourceful, and resilient.

However, that doesn't mean the process will be easy. I'm guessing Noah faced his share of critics, hecklers, and haters. And he probably had to be very patient as he went about crafting a vessel unlike anything that had ever sailed the seas at that time. Don't you wonder if Noah worried about a boat that big springing a leak? Or maybe that was just one more thing he had to prevent as best he could and then leave to God. Maybe Noah was the first person to coin that old saying, "Hope floats!"

His faithfulness in fulfilling God's dream for his life certainly gives us all hope. Because I find it very encouraging that when the rains began and the floodwaters rose, Noah was six hundred years old (see Gen. 7:6). I can't imagine building a ship in a bottle at one hundred, let alone building an ark at age six hundred! If Noah had to wait that long before he saw his ark set sail, then you can rest assured it's never too late for you to finish and launch your dreams.

Color Your Dreams

During the time when Noah was building the ark, however many years that must have been, I'm guessing he had some kind of blueprint he had devised based on God's instructions. Or maybe he didn't need one because God allowed him to remember it all as precisely and accurately as it needed to be. But I suspect most of us need to begin the process of saying yes to our Destiny by expressing our dreams in words.

I'm a firm believer in the power of writing down your dreams. It's the first step in taking them seriously and acknowledging your belief that they will come to life. Something happens when you put your dreams on paper. Your vision and goals begin taking shape in concrete form. The Bible gives us a major success key in Habakkuk, "Then the LORD told me: 'I will give you my message in the form of a vision. Write it clearly enough to be read at a glance. At the time I have decided, my words will come true. You can trust what I say about the future. It may take a long time, but keep on waiting—it will happen!'" (2:2–3 CEV).

Once you have your dreams in written form, I encourage you to start adding images and illustrations. Cut out pictures from magazines, draw and sketch, take pics on your phone—whatever you feel inspired to do that provides visuals for your dreams.

There's no right way to create what I call a "vision map." You just need to experiment and capture as many expressions of your dream as your imagination can produce. Words, images, videos, music, clothing, colors, crayons—whatever works! Let yourself feel like a kid again. Get in touch with that part of yourself you may have had to shut down and lock away because of your grown-up responsibilities. You may be surprised by who you find inside.

In fact, I recently noticed several coloring books for adults on the *New York Times* best-seller list. Apparently, psychologists and doctors have determined that the act of coloring pictures is a great stress reliever. Maybe it makes us feel like children again, but whatever the reason, it's very popular right now. Tap into this same kind of creative, anything-goes, no-right-way energy as you go about describing and illustrating your dreams.

If you struggle to let yourself do something so childish and fanciful, then stop thinking about it and just do it. No one should be watching as you mine the treasure within your heart and create a map to its location. Unleash your imagination and step out of the rational, logical box you live in 99 percent of the time.

Remember when you were a kid how you could finger paint and make the sky green and the grass blue? How you could make up new species of animals or design an outfit for your doll out of aluminum foil? The way you could transform a cardboard box into a spaceship, a beauty parlor, or a clubhouse? Liberate your childhood imagination and discover the color of your dreams.

Here's one example of how this practice works for me. Whenever I am dreaming about my next airplane or car acquisition, I will purchase a small collector's model of it and set it on my nightstand, my desk, or the bathroom counter—wherever I will see it most often. Through this miniature version of my next "big boy toy," I am sending a message to my mind and heart that this item is in my future.

For example, I recently purchased a red "monster truck" that I have been dreaming about for seven years. But I'd had it growing in my imagination long before I made my actual pur-chase through the small collectible version sitting on my desk. Every time I looked at the model I would smile and remind myself that my wonder toy was on its way to my driveway. At the time that I started dreaming about the truck, it was light-years out of my budget! But that did not stop me from test-driving it, taking a selfie with it, and putting a desktop model within my eyesight. Over time the truck came down in price, and my income rose, and I was able to buy my dream truck for pennies on the dollar.

Discovering Your DESTINY

- What did you love to do as a child? Play sports? Draw pictures? Read stories? Bake cookies? Make up your own songs? Brainstorm a list of activities, hobbies, and top-ics that you enjoyed while growing up. Choose one of them to do today as a way of unlocking your imagination and reconnecting with your dreams.
- Make a "vision map" that captures words, images, col-ors, and textures that reflect your dreams. You can draw, paint, sew, sketch, and glue pictures from the Internet and magazines. You can make a digital version as a Pin-terest page or create a hard copy out of poster board. The goal is to begin creating something that you can use as a reference, a treasure map, to inspire you to forward-moving action. Keep it handy so you can look at it throughout your day or add to it as new ideas come to you.

This process of expressing my dream goals is something I practice regularly. As a result, I have my vision map that I carry around with me, both in hard copy form in my briefcase as well as a digital version on my phone. This keeps them in front of me on a daily basis and reminds me of their importance. At this stage of my life, I have many dreams on my list that have already been realized, but I replace them with new ones as soon as I can. These are usually goals so big I can't even imagine how they could ever come to pass. But my job is just to dream—and take the next step of faith as God reveals it to me and opens opportunities before me.

My job is to give myself permission to dream, just as your job is to give yourself permission to dream. No one else can do it for you. If you're waiting on your parents or your spouse or your kids or your siblings or your pastor or your boss to give you permission to dream, then you'll never go anywhere. Yes, you need their support and want their encouragement—and we'll talk about that in chapter 7—but permission to dream only comes from within.

You don't have to know how you'll do it or even what the next part of the process looks like. You simply have to be faithful to own your dreams, name them, and give voice to them. You have to listen to God and when He speaks to you—through His Word or certain circumstances or certain people in your life—then you must follow. He placed the seeds of your dreams inside you, and now you're responsible to nurture and grow them until it's harvest time.

BENspiration

What you discover in your imagination will soak
into your subconscious, increase your faith,
and fuel your actions.

Sleepless and Successful

I once heard a story about Jeff Arch, a high-school English teacher and part-time karate instructor for many years before making the choice to pursue his dream of being a writer. Apparently, Arch couldn't sleep one night and ended up staying up channel surfing in front of the TV. Around four in the morning, he was flipping stations and paused on one of those paid infomercials where a motivational speaker was challenging viewers to tell themselves the truth about their dreams.

Something happened inside Arch in that moment as he heard the speaker's challenge—the spark of his dream was fanned into a flame. Arch said in that moment it dawned on him that he was not where he wanted to be in life. He had a good life, a family with two kids, and he loved teaching the sport of tae kwon do. But he had never wanted to run a karate studio or grade high-school essays; it sort of just happened.

So sitting there in front of his TV at four in the morning, Arch vowed to pursue his first love—writing movie scripts. Deep in his heart he had always longed to be a scriptwriter and create screenplays for the movies. But we all know how impossible it is to get a movie made, right? How could a thirty-eight-year-old guy from Virginia get Hollywood to make one of his movies?

Arch had always let the odds keep his dream at bay. But that morning, he made two promises to himself. First, he was going to do something he previously would never have considered and buy the motivational speaker's material. Obviously, the speaker's words resonated and inspired him, so Arch considered this purchase an investment in his dream, in the future life he wanted to live. Second, he vowed to follow through and make himself read books, listen to CDs, and attend seminars by the speaker and any other motivational gurus who would fuel his dream.

He kept those two promises and every day took to heart the messages surrounding him. Within a month, he quit making excuses and wondering how he could ever manage to beat the odds and started writing. Arch had a great story idea and drafted a screenplay, which he then bravely risked sending out to producers in Hollywood. Less than a month later, he was cashing a check for a quarter of a million dollars for his screenplay, a now-classic romantic comedy called *Sleepless in Seattle*. If you haven't heard of it, just ask any woman over forty!

His screenplay went on to be nominated for an Academy Award and led to Arch's dream of becoming a full-time scriptwriter and movie producer. He beat the odds by listening to his heart on a sleepless night, and it's not a coincidence that his movie's main character does the same. "Don't let anything stand in your way, be the first," Arch advises.

Dreaming into Doing

Success stories like Jeff Arch's remind us to risk our hearts and be honest about what we really want in life. They remind us God's plan for our lives is far bigger than we usually imagine (see Eph. 3:20). It's just a matter of exploring within yourself and examining what gets you excited and identifying your unique gifts and talents. As you explore your likes and dislikes, your passions and persistent pursuits, think about what fans that pilot light inside the furnace of your soul. Chances are good that even the things you loved doing in childhood reflect your purpose.

At the age of three I was banging on my mother's pots and pans and created my own little drum set. Mom says she knew I was a born musician and never complained about the loud noises I created with the pans. Later on in life she got me a mini drum set for Christmas. In school I excelled in the band as a drummer and tuba player, and received almost two dozen college scholarship offers for music when I graduated high school. Because I was also a six-foot-six-inch gifted basketball player, I had just as many offers for athletic scholarships. Consequently, I got distracted from my true love—music—and accepted a basketball full-ride scholarship in an effort to "go pro" and go after the big money.

My story took a tragic turn, which I'll share in detail in the next chapter, and my NBA career got cut short before it really started. As I struggled to overcome this major disappointment, I eventually heard something inside myself—a new kind of hybrid music that's now called gospel jazz. I had never heard anything exactly like it, and I didn't know how to go about establishing a music career or even beginning the process. But I knew I had a big dream tethered to my passion for music. So I began to do my part by honoring what God has given me by just taking the next step.

Looking back, I see how the dollar signs of playing pro ball clouded my vision. Plus, I received tons of attention and affirmation from my family, friends, and coaches to pursue a career in the NBA. Pretty soon, I was telling myself that it was what I wanted because my love of music had been pushed aside.

This is often the challenge we face growing up. Usually we don't know ourselves well enough to identify and pursue our greatest passion. So we listen to those around us and try to do what they tell us we should do. Or we listen to the message that we can do anything and everything we want, which is simply not true. We may have lots of options, but reality has to be factored into the process.

In fact, I don't think we should tell our kids they can grow up to be anything they want to be. I think we should give them the tools and support to discover what they were designed to be by God. If God made me to be a musician, I would have wasted years trying to be a basketball player. Once my purpose was clear, it empowered me. It's not uncommon for me to compose and record music for twenty-four hours straight and have to drag myself out of the studio for meals and a shower.

When you are pursuing your purpose, you are naturally happier, sharper, more forgiving, and expectant.

So what is the deepest desire of your heart? Just go do that, because what the world needs is you . . . the real you. Expectation gets you out of bed in the morning. It causes you to focus on where you are going and not where you came from. What is the deepest desire of your heart?

If you can't answer that question there's a good chance you're living your life merely as a reaction to what happens around you. Too many people are thermometers in life instead of thermostats. I have learned that successful people all share these important distinctions: They know what they want. They are sure of it. They live it on purpose. They know what makes them tick, and therefore they know where their GPS points are.

What is that one thing that, when you are doing it, causes you to lose track of time? What do you do that gives you great pleasure and a sense of purpose without regard to what you are getting paid? What are you a natural at doing? When do you feel alive in the process of doing something you're good at doing?

If you want to live out your God-given Destiny, then you need to know. And once you know, then it's time to turn your dreaming into doing!

BENspiration

"We must let go of the life we have planned, so as to accept the one that is waiting for us."

—*Joseph Campbell*

Become an Imagineer

No one embodies the combination of dreaming and doing, of imagination in action, more than the legendary Walt Disney. A creative goal had to seem impossible before he would consider it worth pursuing. He would often come into his studio with an idea for his team only to have them shake their heads and say, "But, Walt, that's impossible—nobody's ever done it before!" Disney took this as a stamp of approval that it was worth exploring. On the other hand, if his creative team liked his idea and explained how they would bring it to life, he would often scrap it as not worthy of his standard of excellence.

Disney coined a term for the way the creative process requires both imagining and engineering. He combined the two words to create what he called the "Imagineer," a hybrid of both artist and technician, of dreamer and doer. He knew that it didn't matter how amazing the dream was if there was no follow-up to bring it to life. So he surrounded himself with team members who embodied both a creative spirit and a strong, can-do attitude and work ethic. The results? Iconic cartoon characters, timeless and classic films, and destination theme parks, the "happiest places on earth" where it seems dreams can indeed come true.

Our time together within these pages is about empowering you to enjoy a Full Tank Life. Before you can do something, you've got to imagine yourself doing it. Before you can have something, you've got to imagine yourself having it. Before you can be something, you've got to imagine yourself being it.

Napoleon Hill said, "If you do not see great riches in your imagination, you will never see them in your bank balance!"

How do you use your imagination? You sit quietly and you think, you dream, you see yourself doing something that seems impossible or out of reach. You create descriptions, vision maps, and action plans for what your dreams are and how you will bring them to life. You begin the process of birthing your dreams into reality.

Can you imagine living in your dream house? Or driving your dream car? Can you imagine giving $50,000 to a charity you believe in? What about vacationing in France, Italy, or Australia? Can you imagine publishing your book and having a book signing? Or performing a concert in front of ten thousand people?

If you *can* imagine it, you are one step closer to having it. The Bible tells us, "So we fix our eyes not on what is seen, but on what is unseen, since what is seen is temporary, but what is unseen is eternal" (2 Cor. 4:18). Your imagination has the power to impact eternity for God's kingdom and for the betterment of all the people around you.

If you can dream it, God can do it! Unfortunately, many people have stopped dreaming and resigned themselves to cruising on autopilot or to flying scared on an empty tank. We've stopped using our childlike wonder and the power of our imagination. I want to challenge you to devote time today to sit quietly and just think. Let yourself daydream. Imagine at least one area of your life being "dreamatically" different. It could be your finances. Your job. Your relationships. Your start-up. Your novel. Your fashion line. Your movie. Your life with a Full Tank!

Just imagine it.

Your DESTINY Diary

Make an appointment with yourself, for at least an hour, sometime during the next twenty-four hours. Honor your dreams by keeping your appointment and going somewhere you will not be interrupted or distracted by work, family, friends, and other responsibilities. Turn off your phone and unplug as much as possible for this sacred time with yourself and your dreams.

To get started, spend about fifteen to twenty minutes just relaxing and thinking about the dreams inside you that need rekindling. Then finish the following sentences as honestly as possible without stopping to judge your responses.

- The one dream that seems to rise to the top of my consciousness today involves...

_____

_____

_____

- This dream surprises me because...

_____

_____

_____

- The last time I thought about this dream was...

_____

_____

_____

- Thinking about this dream makes me feel...(Excited? Nervous? Afraid? Anxious? Discouraged? Inspired? All of the above? Other emotions?)

_____

_____

_____

- The one action I can take today toward exploring this dream is...

_____

_____

_____

CHAPTER 2

DREAMS—The "D" in DESTINY

Filing Your Flight Plan to Fulfillment

Spreading your wings still requires a flight plan!

I can still hear the screams from the stands during my glory days as a star basketball player in high school and college. "Shoot the ball, Tank!" my friends and family would shout. Their enthusiastic support fueled my drive to be the best athlete on the court I could possibly be. I not only wanted to excel so our team would win, I wanted to win so that I could fulfill my dream of going pro.

When you're black, poor—I mean seriously *poor*, and six foot six by the time you're in sixth grade, your environment begins to suggest your future to you. As much as my parents loved me, times were hard for us in the rural ghetto of central Florida. Everyone I knew told me to pursue sports if I wanted a shot at a better life. As much as I loved playing tuba in the school band, I knew that I had to devote myself to basketball if I wanted to succeed (when was the last time you bought a tuba album?). And

I was determined to leave collecting aluminum cans, shoveling chicken manure, and washing dishes at fast-food joints behind forever.

By my senior year I was considered a star player for the Chattahoochee High School Yellowjackets. With my continued participation in band, decent grades, and exceptional athleticism, I was offered twenty-three different basketball scholarships to various colleges before choosing to play for Wallace State, a small college in nearby Alabama. I reasoned that I could get plenty of playing time on the court and still be close to home so that I could visit my family on the weekends.

My dream had always been to use my college performance as a launching pad for a professional career, either in the NBA or in a pro league overseas. After that first year of college, though, I decided to drop out for a shot at going pro right away. I began playing for a pro minor league team, which led me to a shot at the big time: I was invited to an exclusive pro combine where I would demonstrate my abilities and likely be drafted by a team in the NBA. I felt like I had an appointment with Destiny—my dream was on the fast track and about to come true!

The first day of the big event finally arrived and I performed well. Several teams expressed serious interest, and I was elated to realize that more than one team wanted me. After some physical tests of speed and strength, I was selected to play in a scrimmage game that would seal the deal. Virtually every player selected for the scrimmage would be signed to play in the NBA.

I was on my game and all was going well until I went up for a shot, got blocked, and came down hard on the gleaming court. As my knee hit the floor, I heard a *pop* and felt a stab of excruciating pain. The next few minutes, maybe even hours, passed in a blur. But I knew as soon as I heard that *pop* that my dream had just been snatched away. Both my knee and my dream of being the next Michael Jordan were now shattered. There would be no NBA fans yelling, "Tank! Shoot the ball, Tank!"

Driven by Desperation

With my hopes of playing pro ball dashed in an instant, and with no college degree to fall back on, I found myself facing poverty once again. After a few months, my knee began to heal, but I knew it would take much longer for my wounded pride to recover. Everyone back in Chattahoochee, including my family, was counting on me. I had been voted most likely to succeed my senior year—I couldn't return home to Florida as a failure. So I soon found myself living in a little mobile home duplex in Dothan, Alabama. It had no running water and I could barely afford food, let alone electricity.

Up until then I had no real vices—I was too focused on going pro to smoke, drink, or party. But I had a weakness for the ladies, which kept me just as distracted as a drug would have. Where I once felt like I was sitting in a comfy seat in first class, I now felt like Destiny had ejected me from the plane without a parachute! Winter soon descended and I found myself sitting in a dark, cramped room shivering in subzero temperatures. I had no job, no purpose, no life, and no hope of anything changing.

As the old saying goes, "Desperate people do desperate things." Desperate, for me, was deciding to attend a revival service at a nearby Church of God in Christ. I went hoping for some peace, a little encouragement, and a hot meal (maybe these church folks would have some chicken!) but received more than I ever dreamed. Not only was there food and friendly faces, but the joyful worship music also filled something inside me.

Then the minister began to preach on Destiny, and he seemed to be speaking right into my soul. He concluded with an old-fashioned altar call, an appeal for those who needed God in their lives to come down front for prayer. I was the first one to the altar.

Now, you need to know that I had grown up in church; my father was an elder and my mother an evangelist. We had attended various services, meetings, and choir practices almost every day of the week. My parents kept us to a strict code of conservative conduct, which included no movies and modest dress. I'll never forget seeing my two younger sisters swim in blouses and jean skirts!

But something was very different about church on this night. Because I was out on my own and not able to fall back on my parents for support, I had to be a man and stand on my own two feet and take responsibility for my spirituality. That night I surrendered all my pain, disappointment, and frustration, and completely gave my life to God.

Down in front of the pulpit, I knelt as tears spilled from my eyes. While others prayed and worshipped around us, the minister came and prayed over me. He then said, "There's a new Destiny in your future!" and led me to the keyboards behind the pulpit where the worship band had played. Despite my love of music and experience playing the tuba in my school band, I had never played piano. But when I placed my hands on the keys that night something wonderful happened. I began to play like a seasoned professional!

Blessed beyond Measure

Beautiful music came out of that organ that neither I nor anyone else in that room had ever heard. This music sounded jazzy and dynamic, a gospel sound but with funk! I knew I had been anointed by God with a special gift to share something new. Today this kind of music has been recognized as a new style that I call "gospel jazz."

From that night forward I went on to become an instrumental gospel jazz recording artist and producer reaching millions of fans in my new Destiny. Over the years I have progressively discovered and developed many other gifts and skill sets—many of which I never knew were living inside of me. I've become a producer, a motivational speaker, a minister of my own church, an author, a pilot, and the star of my own reality show on Bravo. I've discovered the love of my life, my wife Jewel, and been blessed beyond measure with a blended family of five wonderful children.

Rather than being just a basketball player, now I am a career multitasker with interests and businesses spanning several different areas. I continue to discover that a full life, the abundant life that Jesus promised us (see John 10:10), emerges when you tap into your God-given inner talents and use them to make others happy.

With this concept in mind, I titled my most recent album *Full Tank*. Not only is it a play on words because of my nickname, but I'm convinced the "Full Tank" concept resonates with one of our strongest human desires—to live with peace, purpose, and passion. Fans and listeners apparently agreed since *Full Tank*, my eighteenth gospel jazz album, became my best-selling one.

After many sold-out national concerts, and thousands of testimonials, awards, and nominations, and chart-topping record sales, I decided to write this book, *The Full Tank Life*. While my music inspires you with a smooth jazz soundtrack for your life's road trip, I want this book to serve as your GPS as you journey to your divine destination. I certainly don't have all the answers or know any magic formula, but as I've already mentioned, I want to share seven keys to start your engine and fuel your dreams for a Full Tank Life. Let's get started!

BENspiration

"A dream doesn't become reality through magic; it takes sweat, determination and hard work."

—*Colin Powell*

Your Future's Listening

Destiny is a personal journey, not a destination.

There's a big difference between deciding what you want to be when you grow up and discovering what you were created to be on the earth. When you find out who you are, you will inspire people around you to be their best. Your relationships will improve as well as your quality of life.

After my injury and departure from basketball (which I had *decided* would be my Destiny), I *discovered* my true Destiny by attending that church service. Who would have thought I would end up at the keyboard that night, playing like a seasoned professional jazz musician! I knew right then that music was my life calling, something I was made to do, uplifting people through words and music.

As transformational as that night at church was for me, everything didn't improve overnight. I still had a lot to learn, and I'll share many of those educational experiences with you in the pages to come. But for now let me remind you of something you already know. If you're going to have a Full Tank Life, if you're going to be fulfilled and at peace, then it will be because of what *you* do, not what others do. No one can discover and experience the joy of living out your Destiny but you. Your future only listens to one voice—*yours*! As I frequently tell myself, "If this is to be, then it's up to me!"

No matter where you are in life, you still have choices. They may not be the options you want and they may not exist under the best circumstances, but you always have the power to choose how you will respond—to events, to people, to your own thoughts and emotions. Right now you have the power to choose what to do with the rest of your life.

You're reading this book at this time in your life for a reason— it's the collision with Destiny you've been waiting on! Don't settle for what you think you want when you can discover how to fulfill your deepest longings—what God created you to do during your precious time on earth.

Determine Your Destination

As a pilot I have learned many life lessons related directly to flying, and perhaps none is more important than the significance of having a flight plan. When I'm planning to fly, I have to notify air traffic control, the ATC for short (who I think of as "the boss") about several things: the departure point, type of aircraft, registration number, destination, number of people on board, anticipated average speed, amount of fuel, estimated time en route, direction or flight path, and estimated time of departure as well as arrival. Sounds like a lot, I know, but every item is crucial to the success of a flight.

Virtually all of these areas correspond to the plan you need to make if you're going to ever get off the ground from where you are now. You need to be honest about where you are and take responsibility for how you got there. You also need to be just as honest about where you want to go; your destination may sound impossible based on your present location, but don't let that stop you from developing your flight plan. You need to think about how you'll get there, what and who you need along the way, the kind of fuel that will sustain you, and how you'll know when you've arrived.

Basically, you need to define success on your own terms. A good way to start is by answering the questions below. Your answers to these two questions should help you verify or clarify your God-given purpose in life.

Discovering Your DESTINY

What makes you *tick*? In other words, what are you good at, what do you think of all the time, what is easy for you without having to think about it? For example, since I was a child, I've always loved music and the powerful way it can encourage and uplift others. No surprise then that music and motivation are huge parts of what makes me tick. How about you? What energizes, excites, and inspires you?

_____

_____

_____

What makes you *ticked*? What angers you? What agitates you? For instance, if you talked to some commercial cleaning service entrepreneurs, many would tell you they hate to see things dirty. For me, I hate the despair, despondency, and deprivation of poverty. I cannot stand to see homeless people hungry on the street, so a large part of what motivates my success is being able to help those in need. So what bothers you enough to do something about it?

_____

_____

_____

A flight plan is like your "vision map," a way to see the big picture and how the smaller pieces all connect together. It's no accident that a pilot's flight plan follows a standardized format so that any pilot or air traffic controller could read it and understand it. However, the pilot must determine the destination before the flight plan can come together. You have to figure out what you want out of life and what will make you happy and fulfilled. I can't decide what makes you tick, what makes your heart skip a beat, or what causes your imagination to run wild. Your family and friends can't decide what makes you smile. *You* have to determine your *what!*

Everyone's *what* is different. As they say, "One person's misery is another one's mansion," and "One man's trash is another man's treasure." If you determine your dreams, if you can see yourself a year from now, two years from now, five years from now living the life you want to live in accordance with how you are made, then you will know how to begin filling your tank. Once you get specific about your dreams, then you become the person who attracts those dreams to you. You will no longer have to chase after what you naturally attract.

Too many people get stuck on the *how* before they have actually defined their *what*. You have to learn to dream like a child again. When Jesus told us to become like little children in order to enter His kingdom (see Matt. 18:3), I believe he was including our imaginations. When kids start cutting out pictures and showing parents what they want for Christmas, they are not concerned with the economy, the availability of items, or the family budget. They are not in touch with the *how*. They just know *what* they want and *when* they hope to receive it (by Christmas).

Once you decide *what* defines your dreams, you will know what you need to achieve a Full Tank Life. I have a few steps that will help you get there no matter what your dreams are. If you want a better marriage, better career, better body, better bank account, or just a better quality of life each and every day, then it all starts with knowing *what* you want so that you can create a flight plan for *how* to get there.

If you don't get honest and specific with what you want, what you hope, what your dreams are, then you might as well be a passenger on someone else's plane. To do better you must become better. As a kid you would automatically grow without trying—you didn't have to think about it because it just happened. However, as an adult you must be focused and strategic about growing on purpose. Ask the average person what their plan is for personal growth and you will realize why they are the average person...because they don't have a plan to become better than average.

BENspiration
If you want to discover the secret of one's success, you only have to look as far as their daily routine.

Having no plan is a bad plan. The secret to your life's success is hidden within your daily routines. If I could spend ten to twelve days with you, I would know if you were fueling your life to run on a Full Tank by your daily habits. One of my own habits for the Full Tank Life emerged from my study of many successful people. I researched the lives of millionaires, looking for common denominators that would apply to anyone. One of my most important findings resulted in what I call "self-align by

7:59." Most successful people accomplish more by 7:59 a.m. than the average person achieves in an entire day. This kind of early self-alignment works because it addresses all areas of a person's well-being—spiritual, physical, mental, and emotional.

While you can adapt this to your own lifestyle, here is a consensus of what "Full Tankers" do before 7:59 a.m. each day:

Pray and Praise—fuel for your soul. Start the day fresh with gratitude and communication with your Creator, asking for His blessing on all your endeavors that day.

Exercise and Energize—fuel for your body. Commit to a regular physical activity suited for your abilities and aptitudes. It might be walking, running, biking, swimming, or stretching. In my case I go to the gym and play two or three games of full-court basketball at six a.m. each morning. Then I eat a healthy breakfast to refuel my body.

Read and Reflect—fuel for your mind. I try to read one book a week but at least one a month. If you invest just twenty minutes a day into reading some kind of stimulating educational material, you will bank ten hours a month toward your personal growth. Don't tell me you don't have time for it. Most people spend at least that much time each day surfing the net or checking social media.

Dream and Direct—fuel for your heart and emotional well-being. Each day I listen to some kind of motivational or inspiring CD as I get dressed. Since I have to get ready anyway, I use this time to suit up both physically and emotionally. You might use your time commuting to listen to speakers, teachers, preachers, artists, and writers who speak to your dreams. Most people are in their cars fifteen to thirty minutes to and from work each day. That's over a thousand hours in your car over a four-year period—the equivalent of a college education! Why not make the most of your time to grow toward your Destiny?

It's what you do *every day* that moves you closer to your goals. It's what you save from each paycheck that builds your savings and increases your assets over time, not just one whole check. It's your daily movement and exercise that builds your body strength, not just one workout. I firmly believe 25 percent of your activity produces 75 percent of your results, so if you self-align by 7:59 each day, then you have the most important areas covered!

SELF-ALIGN by 7:59

Think through these categories and what you could do differently each morning:

- Pray and Praise—fuel for your soul:

  _____

  _____

  _____

- Exercise and Energize—fuel for your body:

  _____

  _____

  _____

- Read and Reflect—fuel for your mind:

  _____

  _____

  _____

- Dream and Direct—fuel for your heart and emotional well-being:

_____

_____

_____

Cleared for Takeoff

Even if I have a flight plan on file for my trip (meaning ATC has a record of my intentions), I can't just take off into controlled airspace without permission. I have to get a clearance from the tower, which usually includes instructions as to how I can begin my flight and initiate my plan. Then I have to *write* down the clearance and read it back to the controller to verify accuracy. So a typical call may go something like this (notice we use the NATO phonetic alphabet—"Alpha, Bravo, Charlie," etc.—to avoid confusion over letters that may sound alike, which means my aircraft number, N401BT, gets read aloud accordingly):

BT—Good morning, November 401 Bravo Tango has information Charlie and requesting clearance to ATL Atlanta Hartsfield.

ATC—November 401 Bravo Tango is cleared to ATL as filed. Climb and maintain 3,000 feet, and expect 10,000 feet within 15 minutes. Clearance frequency is 126.8 Squawk 5657, over?

(I am now required to read back what was given to me. In other words, the controller is not sure I heard him correctly unless I read it back in its entirety. I can't just say "Okay" or "Uh-huh.")

> BT—November 401 Bravo Tango is cleared to ATL as filed. Climb and maintain 3,000 feet, and expect 10,000 feet within 15 minutes. Clearance frequency is 126.8 Squawk 5657.
>
> ATC—November 401 Bravo Tango your readback is correct. You are cleared for takeoff. Time now 21:35 Zulu. Clearance VOID if not off by 21:45 Zulu.

Did you catch all that? In other words, I'm cleared to take off and fly to three thousand feet and can *expect* higher within fifteen minutes. Notice that I did not get *all* I wanted just because I asked for it. I was given a conditional clearance. That means if I take off now (within the next ten minutes), I have permission to fly to three thousand feet and can expect to be cleared for the altitude that I filed for (ten thousand feet) within fifteen minutes. In other words, sometimes the boss wants you to get started on your flight plan, even though you are not cleared for everything that is on the plan . . . *yet*. You may have to start out slow and then pick up speed and climb to a higher level or altitude.

Notice that another part of the clearance says, "VOID if not off by 21:45 Zulu." This means there is a time-restricted window for me to take off. If I don't take off within the time limits given, my entire clearance will be voided, and I'll have to start over. When planning how you will rekindle, pursue, and achieve your dreams, you have to make sure that it's the right time for each step along the way. If you miss certain windows of opportunity, then you may have to wait and start over again. Timing is everything.

You definitely want to seek and follow God's timing. If you are truly living out the purpose He has given you, then His timing is crucial to your ability to exercise your talents and enjoy your life. The Bible tells us that there's a time for everything to happen according to God's purposes (see Eccles. 3:1–8). We tend to grow impatient and have to remember to wait on His appointed time for every harvest. Usually we think of patience as simply enduring the wait time until we get what we want, but Scripture tells us patience means to hold steady and to remain consistent in our faith, believing with confidence that God's promise will bring forth fruit (see Heb. 6:12, 15; Luke 8:15).

When your timing seems off—or more likely, when you're out of sync with God's timing—then it's tempting to quit and resign yourself to disappointment and old thought patterns of defeat. But you can fight the temptation to quit by learning how to wait on the Lord. God's Word tells us, "Though it tarries, wait for it because it will surely come" (Hab. 2:3 NKJV). By waiting, you'll receive your promise in due season (see Ps. 145:15; Ps. 104:27; Job 14:14).

How do you wait on the Lord? Waiting doesn't mean you remain idle. It's like being a waiter in a restaurant—giving God your complete attention and devoted service. While you're waiting, you serve Him with worship and praise. You pray and remain alert for the sound of His voice and what He wants to tell you. And keep in mind that just because He hasn't revealed the right time for your flight to take off doesn't mean He doesn't want you to fly! "But those who wait on the LORD shall renew *their* strength; They shall mount up with wings like eagles; They shall run and not be weary; They shall walk and not faint" (Isa. 40:31 NKJV).

Your DESTINY Diary

Write out a flight plan for your biggest dream, the one you've carried around inside of you for as long as you can remember, the one God planted in you and has made a core part of your purpose. Use the following categories to help you.

- Your present location/point of departure:

  _____

- Description of your dream:

  _____

- Resources needed to get started:

  _____

  _____

  _____

- Resources needed to fulfill your dream:

  _____

  _____

  _____

- People who support your dream:

  _____

  _____

  _____

- Estimated time to fulfill your dream:

  _____

- Ways to measure the success of your dream:

  _____

  _____

  _____

- Other flight plan details needed for your dream:

  _____

  _____

  _____

CHAPTER 3

ENVIRONMENT—The "E" in DESTINY

Preflight Check for Weather Conditions

Your environment will change you before you change it . . . so don't be afraid to go above when you can't go forward!

When I ask people what blocks them from achieving their goals, one of the responses I hear most frequently is "my environment." They will tell me how they could be starring on Broadway or launching their own business app or running for office if they could only change their circumstances, their surroundings, and the atmosphere of negativity produced by others. As I question them, they tell me it feels like going against the current and trying to swim upstream. They know their desired destination, but they can't see how to get there from where they are now. Their path is blocked and they feel trapped.

Believe me, I understand what this feels like! I've sat in a cold, dark room without electricity, hungry and angry, frustrated and furious that my life was not going according to my plan. After working as hard as possible in high school and college, my life-long dream to be a multimillionaire NBA star crumbled with the *pop* of my knee at a pro combine camp. But let me be honest with you. I was not extremely disappointed about not playing pro basketball anymore; I was disappointed about the *money* I thought I would be missing. I liked basketball but did not love it with the passion you see in Magic Johnson, Michael Jordan, and LeBron James. My only reason for pursuing basketball was for the financial security it would bring.

However, I *did* have a strong love for music. But there didn't seem to be a financial future in it. See, I came from a very poor home, and I was six and a half feet tall by the time I was in the sixth grade. Therefore, my height *and* my environment screamed out that my Destiny must logically be a career in pro basketball. As the tallest one in the class (I got tired of being asked, "Were you held back a grade?"), I would find myself stooping and lowering my body to "fit in" with the rest of the world, which was shorter and less conspicuous. So I spent the first part of my life trying to *not* be tall. In other words, I was not standing tall.

It was only after my career-ending injury that I discovered my true Destiny, as described in chapter 1. Attending that Pentecostal revival service (and hoping to get a free chicken dinner), I found a divine gift—to play keyboard, compose, and produce music. Under the Spirit-led instruction of the minister, I sat down to the keyboard and begin to play the first time like a professional jazz musician! It was amazing!

Honestly, I don't know if the gift started that night or if it was already in me the whole time, and I may never know. But what I do know is that I was chasing a basketball my entire life, and continuing on that track, I might have drowned out the inner voice that was inside that was singing a different song. Now, several Grammy, Stellar, and Dove Awards later, with fifteen gold and six platinum albums on the walls of my home studio, I thank God that he redeemed my tragedy into his trajectory. What seemed like the end of my life's dream was really just the fertilizer for the real gift about to blossom.

And you know what? Had I known as a kid that the gift of music was my Destiny, I would have never dressed out for PE!

Through living out my inner calling, I have still been able to enjoy the fruits of labor that the NBA would have afforded me, and I've even been able to buy an interest in a pro team. However, I am reaching more people and I'm far more fulfilled because I am now doing what I was created to do . . . not what I *thought* I was supposed to do. I firmly believe a child should not be asked what they want to be when they grow up. They should be given the tools and exposure to discover what they were wired for.

Too many times people take the wrong path in life simply for financial reasons and never enjoy life because they are forever displaced. After my NBA dream collapsed, at first I couldn't imagine how I would ever hope to be successful again. Playing pro ball had been my highest goal and measure of my own success for so long that when it evaporated, I struggled to set a new course.

And that's when I attended that church service and discovered the gift of music God had blessed me with. Suddenly, it became clear that I could still reach my goals of success, but it would require me to take a different route. My shattered knee would never heal to the level of strength needed for me to play in the NBA. However, my fingers' ability to tickle the ivories on the keyboard still worked just fine!

I realized that I had to let go of one dream in order to grab hold of another. I would keep running into the same roadblock of personal injury if I insisted on basketball as my only way to succeed. However, if I simply backed up and rerouted my flight plan, I had an entirely new perspective! It's similar to when I'm flying at one altitude and hit a band of rough air that causes turbulence in the cockpit. I have to rise above the rough air and go to a higher, smoother altitude. When you have a goal blocked, you have to rise above and go to a higher, smoother altitude.

BENspiration

If Destiny is a personal journey and not a destination, then environment is a state of mind, not your city and state.

You Can't Get into the Promised Land with a Passport from Egypt

When the people of Israel migrated down to Egypt in order to survive a terrible famine, they never imagined their future generations would end up as slaves. But that's what happened, you'll recall, and we have the entire Book of Exodus to tell us about all they had to endure before God delivered them from Egypt. I think the Israelites' response offers a glimpse into human psychology. First, they're afraid and hopeless, resigned to their present reality and assuming God has forgotten them. Then they begin to trust God, but it looks impossible. Then God does the impossible and they're free! At least, until they start wandering in the desert and doubting God again.

The power of their belief—or lack of it—turned out to be the most powerful GPS force anyone has ever known. It's the same force that impacts our direction today—and whether or not we're truly moving toward our Destiny. In fact, the question I get often is, "Ben, how do I increase my belief with so much negativity around me?" That is a great question because you don't have to go far to experience the negative. When you sign on your computer to check your email, you are bombarded with the top news stories of the day, which are mostly negative. Turn on the TV and you get the same thing. Talk to friends and family... same thing. We get negativity so frequently that we have become highly developed in believing negative things quickly.

It is all done through our *environment*.

But guess what? Through the power of repetition you can retrain your mind (and spirit) toward the positive. You have to change your belief. There is something amazing about the power of belief. You can increase your belief by *saying* what you want to believe. Your heart is trained to believe whatever you tell it to believe, so you have to open your mouth on a daily basis (sometimes several times a day) and say positive things about yourself and your life.

I want you to try a little experiment. Think over and over in your mind for about thirty seconds, "I have a horrible life, I have a horrible life, I have a horrible life, I have a horrible life." After you have said it a few times, just say out loud, "I have a great life, I have a wonderful life, I have family, I have a great career, I have great hobbies, I have great relationships."

Well, what happened? Your mind had to stop thinking horrible things because your mouth was talking. See, your words can take command over your thoughts.

Belief will also give you ideas. When you believe you can do something, fresh ideas on *how* to do it will begin to show up. The plan for your success is hidden behind the wall of your doubt. Take your belief and knock the wall down and the how-to plans will be standing right there saying, "I was here all along, what took you so long?"

When you believe you can do it, the how-to-do-it appears. The Bible says that all things are possible for the person who believes. This is a spiritual law that God put in motion that is as consistent as the law of gravity. No matter what race you are or what income bracket you are in, the law of gravity will work the same for you if you jump off a diving board into a pool. Gravity is a law that will always bring you down. Belief is a law as well. Believe big and big things happen. Believe small and small things happen. Believe nothing and nothing happens.

I like to observe the actions of people and have seen this proved out time and again. The most successful two people I know personally are my friends Joel Osteen and T. D. Jakes. I observe and compare their belief processes to those of two of the most unsuccessful people I know personally (old classmates), and I see the results of the law of belief from the perspective of two extremes. Pastor Joel and Bishop Jakes both believe they can move mountains with their faith. As a result, they are two of the most powerful motivators of all time. My old classmates have always been negative and doubtful; therefore they have not had victorious results.

Those who say they can and those who say they can't are both exactly right. You are the prophet of your own life. What are you saying? Start the day with God's input on your schedule. Your agenda (schedule for today) should be decided in the presence of God. Your daily agenda will create miracles or tragedies depending on whether or not you are led by the Spirit of God. Your inner peace is a signal. Don't make a phone call, an appointment, or a decision unless you are at peace in your heart about it.

Remember: "For as many as are led by the Spirit of God, they are the sons of God" (Rom. 8:14 KJV).

In the presence of God your belief level will increase. Disbelief is negative power. When the mind disbelieves or doubts, the mind attracts "reasons" to support the disbelief. Think doubt and fail. Think victory and succeed.

BENspiration
"The first step toward success is taken when you refuse to be a captive of the environment in which you first find yourself."

—*Mark Caine*

Think Small—in a Big Way

So many times people bite off more than they can chew when it comes to dreaming. Sometimes big dreams can paralyze you into inaction because the goals are so big that you won't even try to do anything to get started. Therefore I believe you should break those dreams down into bite-sized goals that you *can* believe. In other words, think small more often. Think small in a bigger way. How do you eat an elephant? One forkful at a time.

It is not the one big deposit of your entire paycheck that funds your retirement. It is the small amount out each pay period over several years that accumulates your big balance. It is not your full day in the gym once a year that makes you healthy and in shape. It is your trip to the gym three to four times a week for sixty minutes that creates the body you want.

Consistent small steps will equal big results over time. The Full Tank Life is one sustained over your lifetime marathon, not this week's sprint. You are in it for the long haul and have to pace yourself accordingly. This is why the power of your beliefs—and what you're believing in—are so crucial to your ultimate Destiny.

As far as how we harness the power of our beliefs, I'm convinced there are basically two types of people: thermometer people and thermostat people. A thermometer is a device that measures and reports temperature or a temperature gradient. In other words, it observes and reports conditions.

A thermostat is the component of a control system that changes the system's temperature to maintain a desired *set point*.

The thermostat does this by switching heating or cooling devices on or off to maintain the correct temperature. So, in short, the thermometer observes and *reports* conditions where the thermostat observes and *changes* conditions.

What type are you?

Do you simply report conditions ("I'm bored, I'm angry, I'm depressed, I am unfulfilled, nothing good ever happens to me.") or do you change conditions ("Today is the best day of my life, I am destined for greatness, here are the ten things I am going to accomplish this week within my vision.")?

Belief is the thermostat that regulates what we accomplish in life. People are products of their own thoughts. You are responsible for setting your own set point. Adjust your thermostat today.

We all have a little Thermostat Man inside of us.

As the CEO of our own lives, we get to put that little man to work for us, and it all happens through the *words* we speak.

Let's test it out.

Tell yourself, "Today is a horrible day." This automatically signals Thermostat Man into action, and he produces some facts to prove you are right. He reports to you that it's too hot or it's too cold, business and the economy will be horrible this year, your family will be getting on your last nerve. Thermostat Man is tremendously gifted at what he does because he will use resources that you trust to prove his point. How many times have you started the day in a good mood but after checking your email or texts or voicemail it blew your day? Just turn on the morning news and in a few moments Thermostat Man has got you sold. It is a bad day. Before you know it, it is a heck of a bad day.

But, on the other hand, tell yourself, "I'm going to make this the best day of my life," and Thermostat Man hears you and goes to work on your behalf to change things. Pretty soon you begin to notice the finer things in life like good weather. You say and think things like, "It's good to be alive and healthy." Thermostat Man has the ability to raise your senses toward the positive or Full Tank side of life. Remember when you bought a car and after you bought it you noticed all of the other cars on the road that were the same make and model as yours? Why? Because your senses have been awakened toward that make and model. Those vehicles were there all along around you but you were not tuned in until you got the model in your possession.

Believe in yourself, believe you can succeed, believe God is for you. Your training for the FTL is self-administered. There will be no one standing over your shoulder telling you what to do and how to do it. Only *you* know what things, goals, and dreams inspire you, so *you* have to think the right thoughts to get there.

1. Think *full*, don't think empty.
2. Remind yourself regularly that you are fuller than you think you are.
3. Full Tank Life people are just ordinary folks who have developed belief in themselves and what they do.

When you increase your belief system, some of the rewards you will enjoy will include a deeper respect from your family, admiration from your friends and colleagues, and increased resources and quality of living.

BENspiration

Belief is the thermostat that regulates
what we accomplish in life.

Discovering Your DESTINY

What have you assumed is the dream you're pursuing? What
roadblocks have you encountered in pursuit of fulfilling this
goal? Do you still have the same passion for this goal you
once had? Could your barriers be pointing you in a different
direction? How so? What might this new direction be?

_____

_____

_____

We discussed your purpose last chapter, but it's a primary
variable I'll return to frequently. For now, consider this:
What dream would you chase if money and financial success were not part of the equation? How does this pursuit
compare to the main goal you spend the most time and
energy chasing?

_____

_____

_____

Avoiding Dead Ends—The Full Tank NO

I used to want to know what successful people *did* that made them so successful. Then I learned that the more important question is, "What do they *not* do?" I believe success is all about saying what *not* to do or what to say no to.

For example, I have clear goals for myself, my music and speaking career, and my ministry. I know that my God-given priority is to make an impact for the kingdom of God in the United States. Currently, I travel over a hundred times a year around the United States to perform concerts and fulfill speaking engagements.

However, every month I receive requests to play or speak at large venues in South Africa, India, Nigeria, Australia, Pakistan, and more. Although I would like to accept some of these invitations, and I'm very grateful for them, I know that I have to keep focused on the United States. Otherwise, I could miss what God wants me to do by spending so much time traveling to nations all over the world. Therefore, I have to decline these invitations at this time. I have to say no.

Or consider another example. I am a volunteer pastor at Destiny Center Church. This is a church that started in our home as a Bible study group and grew into a thriving congregation that is now in its fourteenth year of serving in our community and in our third building. Our services are on Sundays and Wednesdays. An important part of what I do is mentor the members through weekly messages and counseling. Because I own my own airplanes, I am able to fulfill my concert and speaking engagements simply by getting on the planes and flying to the event, which is usually within a two-hour flight, complete my appearance, and then immediately return home to rest and be refreshed to minister at our church for the weekly services.

The aircraft is a tool that helps me fulfill my career goals and also serve faithfully in my local charity work at the church. However, if I took international concert dates and toured other countries like other jazz artists, it would distract me from my main focus of local ministry and national concerts. Why? Because there is no international travel that is a two-hour flight! Most of these flights are twelve to eighteen hours, and when you go you do it as a tour. Leaving in January and returning in August is not an option for me. It is great for the people that do it, but for me, my answer has to be no.

What I say no to is what will enable me to achieve my dreams. This is true for you, for companies, ministries, and individuals. You will constantly have competing distractions trying to steal your focus! The master skill of having a Full Tank Life is knowing when to say no.

What Do You Need to Start Saying No to in Order to Achieve Your Full Tank Life?

Do you need to say no to moviegoing on the weekends or the overtime hours you're putting in so you can finish writing your new book? Do you need to say no to eating out every day so you can save the money to put toward your debt?

"A double-minded man is unstable in all his ways" is one of my favorite passages in the Bible (James 1:8 KJV). Being double-minded makes you cuckoo and unstable in *all* your ways. Focus makes you single-minded and stable in all your ways.

In life there are always new demands and opportunities pressing in for your time, attention, and money. It is easy to get so busy doing "good" things and contributing to worthy causes that you miss out on doing what God ultimately wants you to focus on.

Sometimes it is a need for money that gets us distracted from our true Destiny and calling. For me it was the game of basketball. Just because you are born poor and are six foot six by the time you are in the sixth grade does not mean you are supposed to become a professional basketball player when you grow up. That is what happened for me. But thankfully, I was injured and cut from the team and was able to discover my true calling, which is music and motivation.

Along the way I have had to stop and refocus because sometimes your passion does not feed you. Sometimes your passion needs to be fed for a season until it grows up, then it can turn around and feed you. My music gift did not produce finances immediately; therefore I took a job as an animal control officer to keep food on the table until my music career took off. Later on the music began to make money for me and I was able to stop catching dogs and produce my music full time, for a living. What adjustments do *you* need to make toward your Full Tank Life?

How can you apply this in your life today? Rather than having seven rooms in your house cluttered and messy, focus on organizing one room. Rather than having ideas for six different books to write, start writing one and finish it (like I had to do with *this* book!). It's better to have one book completed that can affect lives rather than three unfinished books helping no one.

I also want to challenge you to focus on one gift or skill that will help you the most in achieving *your* Full Tank Life today. My good friend Joel Osteen has said how in his beginning days as pastor of Lakewood Church he was overwhelmed with everything he was doing. From pastoring at weddings, baptisms, and funerals, to preaching each week and editing the broadcast, everything was moving too fast. He was trying to do it all.

He finally had to stop and think, "What's the *one* thing that I do that contributes the most to what God wants?" It was the Sunday morning message. He had to stop doing many other things so he could focus on that one skill that impacted the larger vision.

I had to do the same with my music productions. I am considered the pioneer or godfather of gospel jazz. That is the style and the genre where I am gifted and anointed, something so deep within me that I hear music in my sleep. However, I get numerous requests to produce all types of music, from hip-hop to rap and even country. I have had to become highly developed in the area of saying no. Otherwise, I would have mediocre results in areas outside of the gifts with which I've been graced. I have fifteen gold records and six platinum records in the gospel jazz realm only because I was able to say no to the other styles that came calling.

BENspiration

Don't drown in the river of regret. Just stand
up—it's not that deep!

Your DESTINY Diary

Description of your present environment:

_____

_____

_____

What you wish you could change about it:

_____

_____

_____

Environmental roadblocks and barriers to achieving your dreams:

_____

_____

_____

Ways you can change your environment to be more positive:

_____

_____

_____

One item you can change right now:

_____

_____

_____

CHAPTER 4

SUBCONSCIOUS—The "S" in DESTINY

Setting Your Internal GPS for Success

Your life's focus naturally expands and becomes an automatic part of your life. Control your default settings so they don't control you!

Think about the last time you drove home from work or your nearest grocery store. You probably don't remember stopping at every traffic light, obeying each street sign, or switching on your turn signal, but you probably did all those things and many more. The route has become so familiar that you do it on mental cruise control.

If you're like me, however, you didn't achieve this ability overnight. When I first started learning to drive, it took all my concentration to focus on driving. Both hands on the wheel, no radio please, keep the windows rolled up, and don't talk to me!

Over time, and through the repetition of driving familiar routes again and again, I became highly skilled at driving without having to break out into a cold sweat every time I turned the ignition. Gradually, my subconscious mind was able to take over the complex system of neural interactions required for me to drive, which freed my conscious mind to focus on other important matters such as changing the radio station, scoping the drive-thru line at Mickey D's, and eating a burger.

With my subconscious mind taking the wheel, my conscious mind did not have to concentrate on stopping at all the lights, remembering to obey every single traffic law, and flipping on my blinker to signal an upcoming turn. Those duties were now taken care of by my subconscious. I could relax enough to trust my subconscious and allow my conscious thoughts to focus elsewhere.

How did my subconscious—as well as yours—learn how to drive? It's actually very simple. By mentally pushing the repeat button each time we got in the car and performed a series of related actions over and over again. With our mind, vision, hands, and feet repeating the same kinds of related tasks, their synchronicity became second nature.

This same habit-forming ability can be put to good use in our pursuit of the Full Tank Life. If we break our desired goals into smaller parts, pieces, and actions, then they become second nature to us and over time result in much greater, cumulative results. We can train our subconscious to work toward our goals through repetitive actions in the right direction.

Your mind doesn't care if the actions are wrong or right; it simply trains your subconscious with the information fed to it at regular intervals. This explains why addictive habits are so hard to kick because the root of these actions anchors itself under the surface, buried deep in one's consciousness.

Granted, I'm not a psychologist, psychiatrist, or expert of the mind by any means, but I *do* have a Full Tank Life, and I believe I can help you get there with a simple understanding of your subconscious mind. If you can train your subconscious mind to gravitate toward the positive goals and habits you want in your life, then you can live your life on "autopilot" 24/7. You don't have to think about what you want to do every day or at every juncture of decision-making. You've already decided.

BENspiration
Your subconscious makes up your mind before you do—so be careful what you feed it!

Sweet Dreams

We have all experienced dreaming at night and perhaps the dream showed you falling and you woke up in a cold sweat. I have often wondered what caused my consciousness to believe the dream was so real. How is it that when you are asleep and dreaming that in your dream the phone was ringing but in real life your alarm clock was going off? What perfect timing! How is it that when I was asleep and dreaming that someone was walking up the sidewalk to knock at my door, in real life someone was actually knocking at my door?

The subconscious tends to know much more than we give it credit for. In fact, it's called the subconscious because it's the part of the mind working below the surface of our consciousness. *Sub* means "below" or "under," and like a submarine cruising in the depths, the subconscious has a course that we may not be fully aware of. But it definitely influences our thoughts, feelings, and actions. In this case, out of sight is not out of mind—we may not be completely aware of what's guiding us, but our subconscious has developed default settings to guide our course.

These default settings tend to develop based on our thoughts and daydreams, the people, goals, and events we think about frequently. Sometimes we don't even realize how often we're thinking about something important to us. We simply get lost in thought and then later realize its significance.

Here's another way I learned to understand the power of the subconscious mind. When I was growing up, my mother was very "mindful." Like many parents, she would often rebuke me when I made big mistakes by saying things like, "Benny, where was your mind?" or "What *were* you thinking?" Pretty soon, she made me so aware of my mind's ability to focus that I found my own personal theme song—"If I Only Had a Brain" from the iconic movie *The Wizard of Oz*. I still love this song and even made an instrumental jazz arrangement of "If I Only Had a Brain" on one of my recent CD releases, a major hit.

But that song did more than just remind me to pay attention. In watching the movie so many times (and hearing that song countless times), one scene really stood out to me: when Dorothy and her three friends—the Scarecrow, the Tin Man, and the Lion—have to go before the grand Wizard of Oz in the gigantic ballroom.

As you probably remember, the fire-breathing wizard loomed

above them—powerful, loud, and very intimidating. That is until the dog Toto trotted behind the green curtain on the left side and pulled it back to reveal the real wizard, an average-sized grandfatherly man, pulling the levers and controlling everything. While watching this scene again as an adult, I began to grasp an important revelation about the subconscious. It's that part of the mind behind the curtain of consciousness controlling everything, even when we are not thinking about it. We assume our subconscious to be large, mysterious, and intimidating, but it's really much more accessible, approachable, and understandable.

One important reason we must be deliberate with how we program our subconscious is so it will work in our favor, not unintentionally against us. For instance, have you ever heard a song being played so often you found yourself singing along even though you hated it? You didn't sit down and consciously intend to learn the words of that song, but over time through hearing it over and over you unintentionally trained your subconscious to remember it. So if the subconscious mind can be trained unintentionally, then it can also be trained intentionally!

Reshuffle the Deck

That is good news for you and me because we don't have to settle for the cards life deals us. This means we can develop our faith, set far-reaching goals, and let the power of our daily routine change our lives for the better ("Self-align by 7:59" should be making more sense to you now!). Circumstances do not dictate your Destiny. Life does not get to be the boss of you—your vision, dreams, and goals allow *you* to be the boss of you.

You don't have to be especially smart, super talented, or particularly gifted to unleash the power of your subconscious. Your subconscious mind is subjective. It does not think or reason independently; it simply obeys the commands it receives from your conscious mind. Your conscious mind can be considered the CEO, and your subconscious mind can be thought of as the executive assistant (which we know does all the work!).

The conscious mind commands and the subconscious mind obeys. Your subconscious mind is a 24/7 administrator who refuses to take a day off and never tries to rationalize or emotionalize any of the commands from the CEO. The subconscious simply "gets it done," whatever it is told. Yes, the subconscious can be super stubborn, too, but you *can* teach an old dog new tricks. And if a dog can be taught new tricks, then surely a human being as amazing as you are can, too!

I can feel my subconscious pulling me back toward my comfort zone each time I try something new. Even thinking about doing something different from what I'm used to can make me feel tense and uneasy. This is why I took up flying and became a private pilot at age thirty-five after a life of living with a fear of heights. Now I'm an instrument-rated, twin-engine-rated pilot who's constantly flying to new heights, literally!

To have a Full Tank Life, you must constantly face your fears and stretch yourself. You must push yourself out of your comfort zone. Because all too quickly, your comfort zone becomes nothing more than a rut where your subconscious gets stuck.

Complacency is the greatest enemy of creativity and future

possibilities. For you to grow, to get out of your comfort environments, you have to be willing to feel awkward and uncomfortable doing new things the first few times. There is not one flight I have ever taken that did not have at least a little turbulence; that's just part of it. However, through the repetition of putting myself in an environment that consistently works to take me safely off the ground to higher altitudes, my subconscious has been trained to push through turbulence and to navigate my life higher, faster, and fuller.

BENspiration
Words are time capsules launched from your lips that contain success or failure and will time-release in your future.

Don't Settle for Good Enough

What are you presently doing to stretch yourself? What are you doing to improve your skills? Don't get trapped into thinking that "good enough" is actually good enough! You were created for more than just average. Today is a new day, and there are new heights for you to climb. Pursue what you love and keep developing that new area of your life. Fuel your curiosity about new interests and see where it takes you. Take a class or find a mentor that will help you live skillfully. Increase your talents, be skilled at your work, and stand blessed before leaders and rulers!

Too often, it's easy to get stuck in a rut, doing the same thing the same way over and over every day. But if we are going to live at our absolute best, we should constantly be growing and sharpening our skills. We should strive to learn and grow every single day because when you stop learning, you stop growing. When you stop growing, you stop living.

To avoid getting stuck in a rut, you must consciously cultivate new interests that stimulate your mind, your imagination, and your curiosity. One of the greatest traps of an unfocused subconscious mind is clutter. And when I say clutter, I mean every kind—physical, emotional, psychological, and spiritual. Scientists and researchers have long identified a clear link between a messy environment and a cluttered mind.

It makes sense, doesn't it? Clutter blocks success. It prevents you from reprogramming your subconscious the way you want because it's already crammed full of so many other odds and ends. If your desk is cluttered, it's hard to prioritize projects and know where to focus your energy next. Multitasking is impossible when you can't locate the individual tasks you want to juggle!

My mom was somewhat of a hoarder. She would pile clothes up on the bed and save every scrap of material she got her hands on. I think because we didn't have much, she figured that having more of anything was a good thing. While I understand the deprivation that motivated her, I still maintain that being unorganized prevents a person from having the clarity needed to pursue their dreams.

So often we think we need more time to get everything done that we want to do, but actually we simply need more space. We need room to move, to think, to grow, to experiment, to fail and to get up again. It's like replanting a rosebush from the container it came in. If it's healthy, then the container is probably overflowing with the plant's roots. They don't have a place to go deeper, so they're stunted. Left in this too-small container, the rosebush will never grow, develop, and blossom to its full potential. Left in an environment that's too small for who you are and what you're called to do, you'll end up frustrated by the constant limitations.

If you want to get started reprogramming your subconscious by giving it room to grow, then start finishing things you start. Begin with small things—making the beds, washing dishes, doing laundry. Finish what you start and take care of what you've got. In the parable of the talents, Jesus sums up his story's point very clearly: "You have been faithful with a few things; I will put you in charge of many things" (Matt. 25:21). God blesses us when we respect what we've been given to do enough to follow through.

One of the greatest challenges I've faced in writing this book is the fact that I have four unfinished book projects! So for years I've tended to chip away at one for a while before jumping to another one and then back again. But as a result, none of them get completed. I finally realized I had to practice what I preach about the subconscious and commit to finishing just one of them. I hope to get to the other three, but I couldn't do them until this one was done.

Unfinished projects take up physical space *and* mental space. Studies show people spend one to two hours a day looking for stuff that is out of place. We all know how frustrating it can be to need a folder on our desk, a PowerPoint on our laptop, or the keys to the car and not be able to find them. We not only lose the time looking for the misplaced items, but we also consume precious emotional energy with negativity. We're either mad at someone else, ourselves, or both!

Unfinished projects drain your energy and steal your peace. It's time to clean up your mess! And you know how I define *mess*? A mess is the dissonance and distance between the way you want something to be and the way it is. You may have a health mess, a weight mess, a relational mess, an emotional mess, a financial mess, or a career mess. And most of us have experienced those times when one mess seems to spread to another area of our lives like poison ivy. If things are messy at home, it's hard to keep things together at work. And if work messes are stressing you out, then it inevitably goes home with you.

Discovering Your DESTINY

Here are some ways to help you clean up your various messes:

- Make a master list of all your physical messes. Go through every room of the house and office and make a list.
- Decide when you're going to get started. I say there's no day like today. Tomorrow is the only day of the year that appeals to a lazy person.
  - Start with the room you spend most time in.
  - Start in the areas that are visible to the eye. This way you can see some progress and be encouraged.

- o Don't skip the small things…the spirit will transfer. If the bed is halfway made, the report will be halfway written.
- Make a master list of all your mental messes. These unfinished actions, unspoken words, and untangled relationships consume precious energy you could be channeling into constructive, productive activities. Unfinished mental projects will nag you and rob you of peace and motivation. Items on your list might include:
  - o calls that need to be made
  - o bills that need to be paid
  - o an apology that needs to be given
  - o a degree that needs to be finished
  - o a degree that needs to be started
  - o life insurance that needs to be established
  - o a will that needs to be drawn up
  - o a book that needs to be written
  - o a business that needs to be given your full attention
  - o an email that needs to be returned
  - o a thank-you that needs to be sent
- Celebrate your progress in cleaning up the mental clutter!

You will be shocked how good it feels to mark even one item off your list! And the more you accomplish in cleaning up messes, the more momentum you create to tackle the rest. So get going and finish something. Don't clog and clutter your subconscious with a hodgepodge of unfinished business and unresolved issues. Make room both physically and mentally in your life for God to bless your new endeavors.

Focus + Mastery = Expansion

Once you've cleared the clutter, then it's time to get down to work. And I do mean down! If you want to reprogram your subconscious, you will need to cultivate three habitual mindsets. These provide keys to igniting your Full Tank Life by resetting your default controls.

Focus. You become what you think about the most.

If you desire an *increase* in finances, you will have to *study money.* If you want an *increase* of love within your family, you will have to *spend more time* with them. If you want to *increase* your wisdom, you will have to *pursue mentors and leaders.* You can't be stuck on the island of "I know enough" if you want to lead a Full Tank Life and fulfill your Destiny.

The main reason most people fail is distracted vision. They have never clarified their life's focus. They're floating, unanchored and untethered. If you want to make the most of your subconscious's ability to guide you, then be deliberate and specific about what you're after. Whether it's a college degree, a business investor, a promotion, a certain way of life, a ministry to the poor, or a loving family, find your focus.

Mastery. Mastery requires you to eliminate possibilities and concentrate on probabilities.

Michael Jordan...Evander Holyfield...Tiger Woods...have all mastered and excelled in their sport. Diana Ross, CeCe Winans, and

Beyoncé have all mastered and excelled in their musical endeavors. Colin Powell, Condoleezza Rice, and Ben Carson have all mastered and excelled as public servants in leadership. It's time you stopped attempting so many projects and mastered one, maybe two, areas.

If you're not sure what to cut and what to concentrate on, get back to Full Tank basics: What do you love? What will get you out of bed in the morning with a smile as you anticipate the day ahead? What you love is a key to something you can master. And the proof of love is the investment of your time. Your time and your money end up going to what you value the most—not what you claim to value the most. So be honest with yourself about what you love and why you love it, and what you're going to do about increasing your mastery in this area.

Expansion. Trust God to guide you, believe in the abilities He's given you, and stretch beyond your perceived limitations.

Once your focus has been established and you're concentrating on mastery, you will naturally begin expanding your world of possibilities. The Bible instructs, "Enlarge the place of thy tent, and let them stretch forth the curtains of thine habitations: spare not, lengthen thy cords, and strengthen thy stakes" (Isa. 54:2 KJV). Expansion can mean different things to different people. For some, expansion is simply following the path you're on in life and moving from one milestone to the next. In order to expand who you are, though, you have to look beyond the horizon and be willing to see past your limiting beliefs about yourself.

Easier said than done. If it were easy, all of us would be sailing off into the sunset. Expansion doesn't necessarily have to mean bigger. It may mean deeper. For example, you may want a bigger house or job promotion, but you may also want to grow more fully as a person, expanding your ability to forgive and to express compassion for another human being. Expansion may be about building a family or deepening your relationships with your loved ones. It's about reaching out past your comfort zone and embracing more of who you are—creating a vision!

And what keeps us from expanding and living the vision of our life? The answer is our beliefs. So if you are ready to drop some of your outdated views about yourself and incorporate a little discipline into your schedule, you just might find yourself developing a better you—a better life! I can't control others' outdated views of me but I can control *my* outdated views of me.

In order to expand, you have to be willing to explore the ways you limit your life. I know for me, one of my issues I had to work through was going from a surviving to a thriving mentality. Because of how I was raised and society's messages, it has taken me a long time to step into the fullness of my power and feel confident about my ability to create. For me, expanding meant changing my beliefs about myself. For you, it may mean learning a new language or it may mean emotionally expanding by taking the risk to love someone. It may mean traveling to a new, unknown place or moving into a new space. Whatever it is, have the courage to step into the unknown and reach for what you want out of life.

Let your subconscious be your compass, your default GPS, so that you are heading in the direction of your Destiny even when you're tired, uncertain, afraid, or momentarily stuck. Look closely at the ways you limit your ability to create, and then look at the ways you can turn it around and start moving in the direction of your desires. Most of the time, we focus on the negative, what isn't working. With the topic of expansion and vision in mind, focus and get clear about your limiting areas, not to indulge them, but to transform them and move on.

The motivational speaker Jack Canfield says, "You can't heal what you don't acknowledge." I say, "Bring it up and heal it out" instead of going round and round with the same issue. It's like driving a car. You get a flat. You either get it fixed or buy a new tire and get on your way. Don't stay on the side of the road forever, complaining about your flat tire, pacing up and down the ditches complaining about how unfair it is to have a flat tire—do something about it! If you don't do anything and just sit there hoping it will change—guess what? You'll be sitting there for a very long time.

The same attitude applies to expansion. If you want to create more in your life, focus on it. Give it attention. Do something different. Sometimes life is so filled with challenges, we forget about all the good things happening around us. Part of learning how to expand means focusing on what is good in life, not what isn't working. Do you ever notice when someone gives you a compliment and you take it in, how your body seems to expand and feels really good? And conversely, when someone criticizes you, how your body can tighten?

Courage takes time, so do it scared now and develop guts later on. In expanding your life, courage and risk are key. You have to be willing to risk losing the old part of you that isn't working or that is limiting your life. This is where it can get tricky. Because even though you say you want to change, you also may feel very attached and comfortable with this part of your life. Expanding means saying good-bye to the old. Vision without action is fantasy and action without VISION is chaos. You need them both to fuel your Full Tank Life.

So for today, right now, ground who you are in practicality but be willing to expand into the vision of who you are. You may need to do an inventory of the ways you put limits on yourself. Then put into motion a plan to change, either by outside support or by gaining more knowledge.

Focus on what you want to create—setting forth a *powerful* intention. Acting today on the famous Nike slogan "Just Do It," not just saying you'll do it some day, will bring about a better, more expanded you. You have to be willing to step into the unknown and then get excited about breathing it in! This is how to expand and live your *vision*!

In order to have a Full Tank Life you must train your subconscious mind so that it will operate in purposeful alignment with your Destiny. Your subconscious is the autopilot of your life. If you want it to run as powerfully and purposefully as possible, then combine your focus, your mastery, and your expansion to propel you to new heights. How many old routes and outdated directions are you still following? Let them go and turn in the direction of your Destiny. Quit fighting who God has made you to be and start living your most satisfying, challenging, dynamic life—the *Full Tank* Life!

Your DESTINY Diary

On a scale of 1 to 10, how positive is your current "thought diet" that you're feeding your subconscious?

_____

_____

_____

What thoughts do you need to take captive and release in order to focus on more positive ones?

_____

_____

_____

What can you listen to more frequently that will have a positive impact on your subconscious? List specific music CDs, audiobooks, podcasts, or other items you know will inspire you and fill your mental and emotional tank.

_____

_____

_____

Choose at least one BENspiration from this book that reso-nates with you and write it out on a sticky note or index card or on your phone. Read it every day and use it as fuel for the tank of your subconscious by reminding yourself what's true about your dreams.

_____

_____

_____

CHAPTER 5

TIME—The "T" in DESTINY

Knowing Your Divine ETA

Time cannot be saved—it can only be spent—so know how to spend it wisely.

Time can be your best friend or your worst enemy depending on how you treat it.

Recently I was running late for a commercial flight and arrived at the airport only twenty minutes before departure rather than the recommended hour to ninety minutes before flight time. Rushing through security, I knew I still needed to make one more quick stop. At six foot six and 270 pounds, I've learned the hard way that most airplane bathrooms are not NBA-sized, so I usually use the terminal restrooms before my flight.

In such a hurry that day, I didn't see the UNDER CONSTRUCTION signs posted near the restrooms. Instead I dashed in and, not seeing any urinals, headed for the nearest stall and shut the door. In a matter of seconds I heard the *click-click* of high heels on tiled floor as the sound of women's voices rushed toward me. Talk about panic—I was in the *women's* bathroom!

I froze in place and ducked my head so they could not see me above the stall door. I could just see the headlines: BLACK PASTOR CAUGHT IN LADIES' BATHROOM AT CHICAGO AIRPORT! There was only one thing to do, and that was wait until the women left and then rush out and keep going. But every time it got quiet and I thought the coast was clear, I'd begin opening the stall door just as another woman walked in. It would've been funny, like something out of a sitcom, if it hadn't been happening to *me*!

By the time I was able to make my exit without being noticed, an hour had passed! Needless to say, my checked luggage made a trip without me because I definitely had missed my flight. Lessons learned: plan ahead, give yourself a healthy margin of time when traveling, and read the (bathroom) signs around you.

I'm convinced the signs of life are the same way. If we're rushing so fast that we miss crucial information, it will definitely cost us more time, more energy, and more missed opportunities, not to mention potential embarrassment. This incident reminded me that time is our most precious commodity. We cannot stop it from passing, but we can plan how we use the twenty-four hours we have in each day.

BENspiration

If you want to enjoy the Full Tank Life by embracing your Destiny, then you must learn to follow life's lead as you dance with time.

Feel the Beat

When it comes to composing, recording, and performing music, timing is everything. If you have a drummer that's offbeat, it can throw off the entire band. And even just one beat off, only half a second in timing, can ruin an entire production. It's one thing when you're in the studio and have the luxury to keep doing takes until it's perfect but another altogether when you're performing live. And the bigger the venue, the more importance the details of the performance take on.

In big arena concerts or live shows like the one at halftime during the Super Bowl, rhythm determines the synchronicity of the entire production. With the biggest audience imaginable watching from the stands and millions more viewing at home, you can imagine how important it is that every stage tech, every sound engineer, every dancer and extra is perfectly aligned in their timing—if they aren't, it could blow the whole show.

The same holds true for our lives. Bad timing, impatience, rushing into a situation, or delaying your response can all throw your life, goals, and dreams off balance. Taking what I've learned from my music into all areas of my life, I now think things through so time can be my friend instead of my enemy. I've realized that the smallest detail can have enormous impact and make or break the rhythm of your day.

For instance, something as small as putting your keys in the same spot in your house when you come home can save you both time and frustration when you're leaving for an important meeting. There's nothing that will drive you crazy faster than looking for lost keys, a misplaced phone, or a missing purse or wallet when you're trying to get out the door quickly.

My missed flight in Chicago wasn't due to being incarcerated in the women's bathroom; it was because I had planned so poorly prior to leaving for the airport. And soon one domino topples the next and then the structure of your entire day seems to collapse. When you're behind schedule and rushing to catch up, you may not read the signs of the situation around you. Next thing you know, your stress level has caused you to make other errors in judgment because you missed crucial information.

Your Calling Is Calling

When it comes to time, you may feel like you never have enough of it. You may even think it's too late to change your path in life. But that's simply not true! So much of your frustration over time stems from forcing yourself into what you perceive as your Destiny rather than allowing yourself to discover where God is directing you. The Full Tank Life is about having more than enough time for the people you love even as you're doing what you love the most. It's not about scheduling more appointments—it's about divinely appointing what you schedule.

Our lives have a rhythm that often changes with each chapter, each season, even each day. You have to get in sync with the divine tempo in order to let yourself experience the freedom that comes with true purposeful contentment. This process requires patience as well as spontaneity. Some days you must wait for your ship to come in and other times you must swim out and meet it. You must pay attention and know which way the tide is turning in order to swim with the current of your life and not against it.

BENspiration

"Things may come to those who wait, but only the things left by those who hustle!"

—*Abraham Lincoln*

One of the most important ways you can develop this sense of timing in your life is answering your unique calling. God creates each of us as a one-of-a-kind masterpiece unlike any other human being who has ever walked the earth. Based on how intimately He knows us and how He designed us, God places a calling on our lives that will allow us to maximize our time in this life.

You were put on the earth for a specific reason, and you never will tap into your full potential and Full Tank Life until you answer that call. God has an assignment for every single person and a mission that's custom-designed just for you. When you hear God speaking to you about your calling—through certain circumstances, startling conversations with other people, or extraordinary events—you must take notice and listen. The more you refuse to answer, the more out of touch with yourself and your true potential you become.

Or think of it this way. I have a bad habit of not answering my phone. Knowing my voicemail ends with "Have a millionaire day!" one of my friends told me, "Ben, I guess the million dollars is supposed to keep me encouraged until you call me back because you never pick up your phone!" Answering calls has not been my greatest talent. Usually I'm busy with other things and don't want to take the time to stop and talk.

While I'm that way with my cell phone, I try not to ignore the signals of my calling that God places in my life. You see, I've learned once I ignore a call it's easier and easier to delay my response in getting back to the caller. Most of the time I even have legitimate excuses for my delays. But I've also learned sometimes I miss out on opportunities by not taking the call.

Our purpose and passion in life work the same way. If something stirs in you when you utilize your talent to sing, then you must pursue that calling and see if it's leading you to a place in the choir or the top of the Billboard charts. If you love renovating houses and making them look beautiful inside and out, then you might want to consider starting your own business flipping homes. If you're moved deeply by the problems of others and automatically slip into problem-solving mode, then counseling or social services may be careers to explore.

The more you pay attention to the way your heart responds to external circumstances, the easier it will be to hear God's call for your life. You will begin to notice patterns and connections among the various people and events in your life. And if you keep following these bread crumbs of Destiny, you'll quickly discover the path of your purpose. All the more reason to keep your tank full and your motor running!

BENspiration

"We must use time wisely and forever realize that the time is always ripe to do right."

—*Nelson Mandela*

Answering Your Calling

While each person's journey will be unique, I want to offer you a road map that I've found works for most people.

1) Commit to your calling.

Make a decision that answering God's calling on your life is the most important thing you could ever do with your allotted time on earth. You know, they say people live at most eighty to one hundred years. So you have a certain amount of time on earth to do everything you possibly can do to fulfill the calling on your life and then your time on earth is over. Pick up the call. Scripture explains why we feel such completion and satisfaction when we live out of our God-given calling: "I have brought you glory on earth by finishing the work you gave me to do" (John 17:4).

The alternative can be summed up in one word: R-E-G-R-E-T. *Your decision to ignore God's plan or to stop pursuing it will affect you forever.* Keep answering the call and make a lifetime commitment to fulfill this calling. Your feelings about it may change, but if you embrace the calling God has placed on your life, then you can make decisions and take action even when you're impatient, hurting, or frustrated.

How do you get started if you don't hear God calling you or you don't have a clue what to do? Let me share a few of the steps I've incorporated in my life.

First, I believe you have to *decide* to answer God's calling on your life. It is a deliberate, ongoing, daily decision. And the decision is all yours. *God is calling you to pursue His plan for your life.* If you haven't heard it or feel like you've forgotten the sound of His voice, then keep listening. God is faithful and won't start something in your life without equipping you to finish it. Just make sure you're not blocking His call or letting background noise from your life swallow it.

Don't let your past keep you from answering the call.

Don't let people keep you from answering the call.

Don't let finances keep you from answering the call.

Don't let Satan talk you out of answering the call.

Don't let "busyness" keep you from answering the call.

Don't let insecurity keep you from answering the call.

2) Prioritize—and then prioritize again.

Before Jesus stepped out to pursue his earthly ministry, he spent time alone in the wilderness with God. Spending time with God is the number one way to discover His plan for your life. But it's easier said than done because priorities tend to melt under pressure. In other words, you could read this book and say, "Okay, Ben—I now know that spending time with God is the number one priority in my life, and I will make sure I put Him first and start every day with 'self-align by 7:59.'" But then next week your car breaks down and you have to carpool to work and then you have an ushers' meeting at church and your boss wants that report done yesterday. In other words, it's easy to forget about this commitment when the pressure rises.

Don't let your most important goal slip. Stay put. Make time on your schedule. I actually have it on my calendar: *My time with God*. If you don't write it down, there may never be time for it. Don't get me wrong; it does not have to be hours of weeping and wailing, lying out prostrate in front of an altar. It can be as simple as twenty minutes of quiet time in your car as you drive to work.

For me, I like spending time with God with nobody else around so that way there are no distractions. I get up very early, usually at five a.m., to start my day and give God my undivided attention. I treasure that time alone with Him more than anything else that my day can bring. Time with God prepares me for the opportunities of the day.

Spending time with the Lord is the very thing that has brought the most healing to my life. It's built my confidence where I was terribly insecure and feeling inferior. It has given me courage to walk away from things that used to have such a hold on me. It has empowered me to take risks and move boldly into the success of my future. It has truly changed me from the inside out.

Seek Him, talk to Him, listen to Him. If pressure pulls you

away, then start over as many times as necessary. But don't give up on developing your relationship with God.

Consistency is the key to change.

3) Prepare for where you're going.

When opportunity arrives it's too late to prepare. You may have a dream in your heart, but you can't just wait for that perfect day to happen—you have to prepare for it.

Time with God gets you ready for the Full Tank opportunity. But when the door opens in front of you, don't hesitate and miss your opening because you're not prepared to take steps through it.

Many years ago during my private prayer times, God showed me that I would be playing music on stage in front of thousands of people at jazz festivals and gospel conventions. So I began to practice what I would say when I first hit the stage. I knew that if I was boring and just another musician that played instrumental music then the crowd would tune me out and begin to talk all over me like I was a lounge lizard in a nightclub. So I started preparing my presentation to be more motivational. I would step in front of the mirror and say "Good evening, Chicago, let's make some noise!" Or, "Hey, I'm Ben Tankard! You know who I am but I don't know you are. We need to get better acquainted! Everyone scream out your name to me and then go hug three people and introduce yourselves to them. Meanwhile me and the band will get ready for our first song—'Ain't No Stoppin' Us Now.' " I was preparing myself so when I got the call for the big gig I would be ready to answer it.

Are you ready to answer your call? Will opportunity surprise you? Are you able to say that when the opportunity comes you'll be ready? Are you reading everything you can get your hands on about what you believe you are called to do? Is your goal to have your own business or become a nurse? What are you doing to prepare yourself? I believe those instructions come from special time with God. The time to prepare is now...not New Year's Eve or your next birthday!

4) Separate your calling from the expectations of others.

You must please God and not man. If you're going to fulfill God's plan for your life, it may require letting go of some present friendships and relationships. You may have to detach from some people who are dragging you down and holding you back because they don't grasp God's best in their own life.

Remember, the four forces of flight correspond to your life: lift, thrust, weight, and drag. People are going to fall into one of these four categories in your life. You need lifters and thrusters around you, not people who will weigh you down and drag you back to mediocrity.

5) Write your dreams on paper.

Think about all the "how-to" books out there. If "how-tos" were enough to instruct and motivate us, we would all be skinny, rich, and happy. There is not a shortage of self-help books out there, but there is a shortage of people who will actually write down what they want based on what they learn. The "how-to" means nothing unless it gets attached to your "what to." There are no maps to "nowhere." You must have a destination. The Bible couldn't be clearer about this: "Write the vision and make *it* plain on tablets, that he may run who reads it" (Hab. 2:2 NKJV).

It has been proven over and over that people who write down their dreams are more successful than those who don't. Dreams that are not written down are just wishes. I heard one motivational speaker say that one way to write your dreams is to write your obituary. In other words, imagine you're going to live to be one hundred and write out the whole story of your success in your obituary.

Because this seems rather morbid to me, I would rather encourage you to write your own Wikipedia page. This way you can go online and see the wiki page of those people you admire the most, copy and paste onto your paper, move it around, edit with your dreams, and custom-make it into something you can copy and share with friends and family (make sure it is the thrusters and lifters you share it with . . . not weight and drag!).

You have to get your dreams on paper in pencil because they *will* change over time. You may not know *all* of the call of God on your life right now, but just write down the parts you do know. According to a recent article in *Time* magazine, most people don't accomplish the five major things they wanted to do in life. I believe it is because they did not write it down. So write down your Full Tank favorite five and start there!

6) Resist the urge to procrastinate.

Nothing worth achieving comes easily. We're told in Scripture, "In the world you will have tribulation; but be of good cheer, I have overcome the world" (John 16:33 NKJV). In other words, spending time with God, having a written vision, and being prepared does not insulate you from resistance. You must be prepared to fight for your dreams, fight for your family, fight for Destiny, and fight for your Full Tank Life.

Just like with the game of football, the closer you get to your goal, the tougher the resistance. Everyone makes New Year's resolutions but some people give up at that same place every year, usually around sometime in February, when they're right around the corner from a true breakthrough. "Dreams come about with much business and painful effort" (Eccles. 5:3 AMPC). In other words, success is the willingness to bear pain.

BENspiration
You will never outgrow warfare—you will simply have to learn to fight harder. Remember, new levels bring new devils!

The Bible tells us to fight the good fight of faith (see 2 Tim. 4:7). Why? Because if it was easy, everyone would be doing it. Iconic inventor Thomas Edison said, "I failed my way to success." This statement from the guy that invented the light bulb—after over hundreds of prior attempts!

Living out of your calling and remaining in step with God's timing won't be easy. One time we were getting ready to go out on a date, and I dressed first, so I sat at my computer to check some emails while I was waiting on Jewel. I got caught up and lost track of time and did not realize how late it was until Jewel called me on my cell. When I answered, she said, "Honey, come on! We're going to miss the movie."

I said, "I'm ready! I'm just waiting on you." To which she then said, "No, you are not. I'm already in the car, and I'm waiting on *you*!" Sometimes people say that they are waiting on God to get started on their dreams, but God is not *behind* you. He is in front of you and waiting on you!

Anyone can begin a marathon. Champions finish them. Everyone experiences adversity. It is those who stay strong to the finish who are rewarded. Pace yourself. Determine to go the distance. "Yes indeed, it won't be long now. Things are going to happen so fast your head will swim, one thing fast on the heels of another. You won't be able to keep up. Everything will be happening at once, and everywhere you look, blessings!" (Amos 9:13 MSG). Keep your pace and hit your stride. Keep aflame the spirit of a finisher!

Discovering Your DESTINY

Make a list of activities, events, and relationships that would help you pursue your dreams. Choose one of them and make the necessary adjustment to your schedule so you have time for it.

_____

_____

_____

Perform a time audit by reviewing your schedule, your calendar, and all appointments for the past month. Group the ways you spent your time into the following categories: family, work, church, school, friends, resting and relaxing, and dreaming. Which category seems to consume the most time? Which category needs some serious time and attention to help you fill your tank and balance your life?

What's the biggest time waster you battle? Watching TV? Surfing online? Facebook? Something else? How could you limit the time you're wasting so you'd have more time to pursue your dreams?

Tuned for Destiny

One of the most dramatic examples I've experienced of seeing my calling collide with God's timing led to my reality show on Bravo, *Thicker Than Water: The Tankards.*

This show is such a great example of God's progressive Destiny for my life and the way He often only reveals glimpses of your future until it's time for the big reveal. *Thicker Than Water* definitely didn't start out like you see it on TV—it evolved into something bigger and better than I could've envisioned.

The genesis of the show emerged from a local broadcast my wife Jewel and I hosted each week called *Tuned for Destiny*. We paid for the TV studio time ourselves and viewed it as an outreach for our ministry. Sitting at a kitchen table with coffee in the studio, we'd chat and discuss different topics relevant at the time. Before long I started grabbing home video footage of our family during the week using only my iPhone, which I'd edit and show for laughs at the end of our broadcasts. It was a *huge* hit! Viewers loved seeing "behind the scenes" into our family and enjoyed the footage of our home as we went through the daily routines most families experience.

Based on the number of requests and views of my bonus footage, we started posting it on YouTube. From there it *exploded*! People absolutely loved it, and soon we had more people tuning in just to see the hijinks of our family members than those watching for the "serious" teaching discussions Jewel and I taped in the studio. We enjoyed the positive feedback and the joy of knowing so many people loved being part of our family and all our craziness day to day.

But we never expected what happened next. Apparently a producer at Bravo saw our YouTube clips and contacted us about a family show concept. The next thing we knew, thirty people from Hollywood were knocking on our door and our house was full of cameras! We began shooting daily episodes and doing all the work necessary to promote a successful reality TV show— media tours, red carpet events, and meetings with fans. The success of our show is beyond what we could've ever dreamed! And it gives us a platform for a laid-back, more intimate kind of outreach than we could ever have had with our old show.

I've learned so much about timing from taping the show in advance and planning our family events so far ahead. And while great editing helps make the show flow into a coherent story about our lives, I'm constantly reminded to make the most of my time regardless of whether the camera is rolling. Obviously, I now have another huge area of my life to juggle with the show. But I'm also reminded about making the most of my time by the way the cameras reveal who we are.

Making *Thicker Than Water* has taught me that being an open, transparent person is actually a good thing because it helps other people see themselves honestly. I used to think that I joked too much, was too candid and too forward with personal details. I would be the first guy to talk about whatever elephant was wandering around in the room. I would say what other people were thinking but would never say. I'd grown accustomed to thinking these were flaws, poor traits I needed to correct and contain. After we signed on to do the reality show, the producers told me that my characteristics were the very things that made for a hit show. They told me, "Perfect people don't sell."

Viewers of reality TV want people they can relate to, hang out with, and enjoy being with. It's very aspirational because people get to track a real-life conversation in the context of another family, not watch a scripted story. I believe people are looking for answers. Watching reality TV is not only entertaining and relatable, but it is an instructional classroom for life. Viewers get to experience the trial and error of life through someone else's mistakes and triumphs. Their mistakes and gleaned wisdom can save us time on our own journeys.

Release the Pressure

One of the greatest deterrents to living in sync with God's calling and enjoying the Full Tank Life is pressure. That old David Bowie song was onto something about the way everyone feels "under pressure" more and more. The busier we are, the more we feel burdened and beat up. This is when time begins to feel like our enemy, a cruel taskmaster who demands everything without giving us enough energy to do it all. Which only creates more pressure!

We've all got responsibilities, commitments, obligations, and duties pulling us in opposite directions—we're like a wishbone at Thanksgiving dinner. We feel torn about how to spend the limited amount of time we have each day. Which meetings are worth missing your child's soccer game? How can you balance all the hard work required to pursue and fulfill your calling while loving the significant people in your life?

The result is a mountain of pressure weighing us down. Such weights can be paralyzing and cause you to step out of rhythm with your life. For instance, I used to have writer's block whenever it was time to record my next new album. I'd have all these ideas when I was driving to meetings or doing some chore around the house. But the minute I sat down in my studio and the record button lit up, my creative juices would immediately dry up. Which only made me more panicked and frustrated about when and how I would ever be able to create a new album.

Pressure would be on me from the record company to produce the next big hit. Fans would be posting questions like, "When's the next album coming out, Tank?" And then there was the pressure to continue providing for my family by doing what God's called me to do. I knew I was incredibly fortunate to get to do what I loved doing and make a living at it, but somehow this only made me feel more burdened.

Then one day it hit me. If I could have all these great ideas while doing other, unrelated tasks, then why couldn't I unblock my subconscious and immediately use inspiration where I found it? I knew my subconscious remained busy storing up all my music ideas, song melodies, and beats. And you'll recall from chapter 4 how important I consider the subconscious to the Full Tank Life.

So if my subconscious works all the time, why not record my hit when I get it, or when the idea is fresh, rather than waiting two weeks, months, or years later when it's time to go into the studio? Since I have my own studio in the home, there should be few excuses, and I can record anytime the muse strikes, even if I'm in my pajamas.

I had automatically assumed that the only place to write songs and record music was in the studio. Plus, this kind of boundary would keep work from spilling over into personal and family time, right? Wrong! Away from the studio, either I was worrying about having writer's block or else I was relaxing and thinking about some great song idea. For me, dissolving the boundary between work and home has allowed my creativity to flow back and forth. I've also utilized technology more so I can record ideas and melodies on the go, which explains how I came up with one of my latest hit releases, "Right Turn Ahead"! Yep, I was driving across town one day and had a beat turn into a melody that seemed in sync with the traffic around me. When I saw the turn signal of the car in front of me, I knew I was onto something!

I'm convinced creativity is the key to dissolving pressure in your life. Be resourceful! Necessity truly is the mother of invention. Think about what you require to do what God is calling you to do. Ask Him to provide this for you. Trust that He will and look for ways to step outside the box of your usual way of thinking. Solutions to your form of writer's block may be right in front of you. Release the pressure by remembering what you have been given and how far you have already come.

Finally, as you consider your relationship with time, keep this in mind: It's not what you're going through but what you're going *to*. God's plan is progressive, so we rarely get to see the full view for what's in front of us. We simply have to be faithful to take step after step and do what He asks us to do for today—not yesterday. Unless you experience the *now*, the future will never please you. Make the most of the time you've been given. Make peace with the fact that you cannot do everything piled on you in any given day. But you don't have to do everything—just the most important things that pertain to your calling.

This time is your time!

Your DESTINY Diary

Do you usually live by a strict schedule or just "go with the flow"? Being honest with yourself, what do you need more in your life—discipline to stick to a schedule or flexibility to be spontaneous—to create more Full Tank time? Change one thing about your daily routine that would help you balance your time in a more fulfilling way.

_____

_____

_____

When have you recently felt like you were using your time productively? What keeps you from feeling this way more often? Work on accepting your limitations, being grateful for what you accomplish in any given day, and letting go of the voice inside you yelling that you never do enough.

_____

_____

_____

Describe your perfect day, hour by hour, from the time you wake up in the morning until you go to bed that night. What elements of your perfect day are currently in your typical daily schedule? Any of them? How can you include at least one of your perfect-day hours in your day?

_____

_____

_____

How full is your tank right now? What do you need to spend more time doing to pour into your dreams and fill your tank more? What's stopping you?

_____

_____

_____

CHAPTER 6

INSPIRATION—The "I" in DESTINY

Refueling Your Soul with Passion

Once you're truly inspired, your passion will create energy to fuel your vision.

One time I was flying back from Washington, DC, and had asked the fuel attendant at the private airport to fill up my plane. The particular model of aircraft I was flying that day has a unique, hidden reserve tank, and I just assumed the attendant would know about it and automatically fill up this tank as well. But then up in the air around ten thousand feet, halfway through my flight home, I suddenly discovered the hard way that my plane was on empty. I had to make an emergency landing near Knoxville, Tennessee. It was one of those times when I emerged from the cockpit and literally kissed the ground!

Inspiration is the primary fuel we burn in our Full Tank Lives. Whatever inspires you to get out of bed in the morning will sustain your energy level throughout the day. If you aren't connected to your passion and purpose, then you'll feel like you're running on empty most of the time. You will question why you're doing what you're doing and find yourself succumbing to distractions and the agendas of those around you.

The key to enjoying a Full Tank Life consistently is making sure you keep plenty of fuel in your main tank. You have to learn to replenish your inspiration and recognize that it is closely tied to your creativity, your curiosity, and the power of your imagination. This blend of fuel will allow you to find pleasure in virtually everything you do. You will enjoy a level of personal satisfaction and professional fulfillment that makes each day an exciting journey of divine discovery.

In the Beginning

Inspiration is often believed to be divine in origin, an immediate sense of revelation from God's influence. The word itself comes from *inspirare*, from the Latin meaning "to breathe in," or as we might say it today, "to inhale." It's no coincidence that the Holy Spirit is often described as a rushing wind, a breath of fresh air, a cool breeze of comfort. And we see the origin of inspiration on the first page of every Bible.

In fact, the book of Genesis starts with a moment I find shocking: "In the beginning God created the heaven and the earth. And the earth was without form, and void" (1:1–2 KJV). While this verse may be familiar to you, I say, "Hold up! How can something that God created be without form and void?" Have you ever considered this? Why didn't God just speak the entire world into existence—sky and land; water and fire; people, plants, and animals—by uttering a single word? He's all-powerful, so He surely could have, right?

Or consider this. After listing the six days of creation, the Bible tells us that on the seventh day God rested. Does God really need to rest? I don't think so—at least not in the way you and I need rest. But what if the Lord wanted to show us something by the very process he used in the creation of the world, something we needed to grasp for ourselves since we are created in His image? Something we need to know in order to create the lives He designed us for? Could He be modeling a process we're intended to follow? One similar to the way parents show their children how to act?

I'm convinced this is definitely one of the messages of the creation as described in Genesis. Notice what happens on Day 2: "Then God said, 'Let there be light'; and there was light. And God saw the light, that *it was* good; and God divided the light from the darkness. God called the light Day, and the darkness He called Night. So the evening and the morning were the first day" (Gen. 1:3–5 NKJV).

Each day of creation then follows the same pattern. God creates something and then He molds it, shapes it, and refines it before He names it. Genesis 1 describes not only the process God demonstrates, but the natural progression from the creation stage into the formation stage to the naming stage followed by a period of rest.

While it's easy to distinguish six days of creation from the seventh day of rest and conclude we're supposed to follow suit and set aside a day for Sabbath, within each of the creation days there's also an important lesson for us about the creative process and the power of the imagination. The initial creative impulse is the idea stage, the moment when you get the concept, song, poem, business idea, or glimpse of that new invention. The formation stage is when you act and put in motion the necessary steps to bring your creative ideas to life.

However, the gap between creation and formation needs a bridge—a commitment to receive the inspiration, take it seriously, and then do what's necessary to birth your dream into reality. Too often, we're inspired with genuinely great ideas but do nothing to fan the flame of our creative sparks into formation. My challenge to you is the same one I've given myself: to document the creation stage accurately in a timely manner so as not to lose it before you can loose it. You've got to grasp the creative idea in order to take hold and make it real.

BENspiration

"Just don't give up on trying to do what you really want to do. Where there is love and inspiration, I don't think you can go wrong."

—*Ella Fitzgerald*

The Bedside Millionaire

This process of fanning creative sparks into flames of formation requires preparation to receive innovative ideas when they come. In many cases our best ideas come to us when we are not looking for them. Floating in our subconscious, they sometimes emerge when we are on our way into, or on the way back from, a deep sleep. This is why I encourage you to adopt a practice that's been invaluable to me. Keep a memo pad and pencil on your nightstand beside your bed and title it *The Bedside Millionaire*. This way you can capture those rich thoughts and ideas that come to you when you are in a restful state.

Now, granted, all creative ideas are not equal in value. One friend of mine told me he'll wake up in the middle of the night with what feels like a 24-karat genius idea only to read it the next morning and discover something like, *Explore new app for pets to use*. We laughed together, but I told him that while our pets may not use a phone or tablet, their owners sure do. Even in ideas that seem silly or obvious you may discover the seed of a brilliant creative endeavor.

The more you document your creative kernels and dream seeds, the more confidence you will develop. You'll come to appreciate your own uniqueness and realize that your imagination is one of God's greatest gifts. You may not think of yourself as the creative type, but you don't have to wear a beret, rent studio space, or sit in a coffee shop writing all day to be creative. I'm absolutely certain our Creator made each of us to create—just like Him.

Creative Confidence

Think about it—when you drive your car around on an empty tank, you are nervous, you must change your trip course, and you are anxious and uneasy. When you have a full tank, however, you drive with more confidence. You know you have plenty of gas to fuel your journey. Creative ideas work the same way. The more seriously you take them and choose to act upon them, the more your confidence will grow. The Bible tells us, "The LORD will be your confidence" (Prov. 3:26 NKJV). If you seek God and obey His voice, then fear and insecurity will become a thing of the past. Confidence changes everything!

BENspiration

A Christian without confidence is like a jumbo jet setting on the runway with no fuel! You're made to fly but not going anywhere!

I would argue the single most important factor determining whether you experience the rewarding life God has for you is confidence. If inspiration is the gas for your Full Tank engine, then confidence is the motor oil! Nothing affects your ability to pursue all that God has for you more than your level of confidence. It determines your willingness to trust God, especially when you must step out in faith without seeing ahead. Confidence also has a huge impact on *what* you pursue and *how* you pursue it.

Your level of confidence is either holding you back or enabling you to achieve optimal success and live the life God has planned for you. Many people miss out or forfeit the ultimate plan God has for their lives because they struggle with fear, insecurity, doubt, and worry. None of which are descriptions of a person with confidence.

You really do get what you expect out of life. If you expect to be declined, rejected, alone, or overlooked, you will be. Your expectations are a direct result of your confidence or lack of it.

Let me repeat: *you get what you expect.*

Your level of confidence affects every area of your life, including:

The career you choose
The relationships you pursue
The way you carry yourself
The way you communicate
The amount of money you make
The relationship you have with God

If you only knew how insecure I was most of my life, you would be amazed at the transformation that has taken place in me. I am not the same timid, fearful, and insecure person I used to be. From my childhood into early adulthood, I struggled with a stuttering problem. But then as I grew in confidence and knew God wanted me to speak, it was no coincidence that a gifted friend and mentor offered to give me free speech lessons.

Similarly, I used to feel so self-conscious and insecure about my height. When you're six and a half feet tall before you finish middle school, you tend to stand out—literally. I hated the fact that everyone noticed me and often made some joke or comment. "How's the weather up there, Tank?" or "Where's the beanstalk?" were some of the nicer ones I heard. On top of being so tall so young, I hated wearing secondhand clothes or hand-me-downs, never having the cool new Nikes or brand-name shirts and jeans my peers had.

But I learned that confidence—real confidence that grows from a solid faith and a trust in the Lord—does not come from what I'm wearing or how I look. "The LORD does not look at the things people look at. People look at the outward appearance, but the LORD looks at the heart" (1 Sam. 16:7). Confidence comes from within, from knowing God loves and values you and wants His best for your life.

On the other hand, insecurity is a purpose-slayer and dream-killer! It will completely stop you from stepping out into the new things God has for you. And sadly, I recently read that each year more people report feelings of insecurity and low self-esteem. Which makes sense if you consider the pressure to be successful by the world's standards is greater than ever—on TV, through popular culture, and all across social media.

The word *insecurity* means "not firm or firmly fixed; likely to fail; lacking in security or safety, lacking in self-confidence or assurance; not safe from attack." It is also associated with being anxious, afraid, shy, uncertain, unsure, timid, self-conscious, vulnerable, unprotected, and defenseless. Insecurity develops over time through a series of events: when we make mistakes, we feel guilty, we do things we are ashamed of, we are put down or criticized by others, we compare ourselves to others, and the list goes on.

Discovering Your DESTINY

What emotional barriers tend to kill or inhibit inspiration in your life? Fear? Anger? Resentment? Jealousy? Envy? Others? How can you channel even negative feelings into fierce, motivational fuel for your Full Tank Life?

_____

_____

_____

What event in your life has inspired you the most or had the most positive impact on pursuing your dreams? A trip to a place you've always dreamed of? A conversation with someone you love? The advice of a trusted mentor? An encounter with a famous artist or work of art? Something else?

_____

_____

_____

Who are the people presently in your life who inspire you and call out the best in you? What is it about each one that makes you want to try harder and live more passionately?

_____

_____

_____

Unclog Your Engine

In order to have a Full Tank Life you must have inspiration. Your level of inspiration affects all areas of your life including your career, family, friends, and even relationship with God. Inspiration is simply another word for confidence. I love this Bible verse from the Gospel of John: "I glorified you on earth by completing down to the last detail what you assigned me to do" (17:4 MSG). I want your inspiration to grow to a new level in your life. I promise you that God has given you everything you need to confidently live out your purpose in life. You just need to see it and believe it.

A lack of confidence is rooted in fear. Fear will limit you and hold you back from the success you desire. Insecurity is like putting sugar in your gas tank—it ruins the fuel and clogs your engine. It is fear that says, "You're not good enough, not thin enough, not smart enough, not worthy enough, not educated enough or polished enough to succeed." It takes courage to look your fears in the eye and not back down. It requires strength to keep standing and stepping out in faith when your fears cause you to doubt yourself.

Even if your fears have sabotaged the inspiration in your engine, know that it is never too late to become the confident person you want to be and live the life you desire to live. But it will require taking deliberate steps. Outward changes are important, but real confidence is developed from the inside out. Your life will never change until your *thinking* changes. "As he thinks in his heart, so *is* he" (Prov. 23:7 NKJV). When you start thinking differently, you will see results begin to bloom around you.

And how do you change the way you have thought for the past ten, twenty, or thirty years? God's Word makes it clear! "Be transformed by the renewing of your mind" (Rom. 12:2). What do you do to renew your mind? Allow God's truth to soak into your bones and replace the toxic thoughts of fear and insecurity. Renewing your mind is a two-step process. It requires getting rid of the old way of thinking and replacing it with a new way of thinking...about yourself!

I speak from experience—it can be done. First, build your confidence *inwardly,* then practice *outwardly.* Both are important. As you begin to change on the inside, the way you carry yourself on the outside will change, too. Your posture improves, your eye contact is secure, your appearance is attractive, and your vocal tone is solid.

If you never feel like you have enough energy, then it's probably because you're not taking in the right kind of fuel. Certainly it's important to get the proper nutrition and enough sleep, but your heart and soul need refueling on a regular basis, too. You need beauty to excite you, mentors to guide you, and creative endeavors to challenge you if you want to have more than enough energy for your Full Tank Life. Discover what makes your heart beat faster and you've started filling your tank!

In order to build your confidence, you must take inspirational steps that will equip you to step out of your comfort zone and go after your dreams. We each have certain "fuel tanks" inside us, and they can be filled through these inspirational steps. And, based on my experience flying back from DC, I recommend making sure you fill more than one tank so that you have plenty of inspiration on reserve. Here are four major "reserve tanks" of inspiration for your Full Tank engine. Keep as many as you can—all of them if possible—full at all times!

Full Tank encouragement

One of the most powerful weapons at your disposal is the power of words. Words are like extended-release capsules full of positive (or negative) energy slowly being absorbed by your mind and heart over time. Harmful, negative words work like poison to pollute the truth about who you are and what God wants you to do. Positive, healing words produce growth and inspiration. These words can be focused and targeted toward change.

If you don't believe me, try this little exercise. Read these words out loud, and if possible stand in front of a mirror while saying them as if you were talking to yourself. I know it sounds a little crazy or silly, but humor me. Try it and see if you don't immediately notice a difference in the way you feel:

I'm quick.

I'm sharp.

I'm gifted.

I'm smart.

I'm good-looking.

I'm healthy, wealthy, and wise.

See how those words made you feel inside. These are like seeds planted down inside you. Feel the roots growing in your spirit, the roots of inspiration that produce sprouts of creativity pushing through the surface of your consciousness.

Now try saying these words to and about other people and the response is even more remarkable. When you start appreciating people and complimenting them, you can see their shoulders rise to the praise almost magnetically. You become labeled as an encourager and people want to be around *you* to be inspired. Your spoken praise and appreciation will fall like rain on parched soil. Before long, you will see new life sprouting in your relationships in response to your words of love.

Even during our childhood, my big sister Patrice has always been a source of inspiration for me. She would always tell me how proud she was of me no matter how small the accomplishment. Whether I was scoring the winning basket in a school ball game or releasing a new CD of my music, she celebrated my achievement and encouraged me to keep going. This went on for years. Now she has a website and blog called *Notes of Inspiration* where she's an encourager to thousands of people. But it all started with the seeds of inspiration she started planting in me and the rest of the family years ago.

What I am getting at is in order to have a Full Tank Life you must be inspired, but even more than that, you must *be* an inspiration. Life is not all about receiving but also about giving. And this occurs naturally when you're doing something you love, living out of the purpose for which you were born. After all, it's more blessed to give than to receive!

Full Tank service

When I was growing up, my dad would take us to the gas station (known then as the "filling station") and ask for "five bucks of regular." Because in our financial condition it was rare that we were able to afford a full tank of gas. However, one summer we had planned and saved and were finally able to take a road trip to Walt Disney World in Orlando, a five-hour drive from our home and one requiring a full tank of gas. I'll never forget pulling into that filling station and hearing Dad say, "Give me the full service!"

This meant we got a full tank of "high-test," air in our tires, the oil checked, and the windows cleaned. I remember telling my dad that it would be great if we could get the full service all the time. He promised me, "One day, son." I was attracted to the full-service benefits and wished we could use them from that service station all the time.

Now years later that principle still lives in my heart, and I realize that people are inspired by my full service to them through kindness, unselfishness, and politeness. When I offer to wash my wife's car or take out the garbage or fix the sink (hoping not to make it worse), these acts of service inspire her, and in return I am inspired again.

There is an old saying that still holds true: "Actions speak louder than words."

In every society throughout human history, gift giving has been perceived as an expression of love. Giving gifts can inspire and encourage and send a message that expresses your care, consideration, and concern for the important people in your life. Nothing inspires an employee, spouse, coworker, or family member like a surprise gift chosen uniquely for them.

Full Tank attention

Giving people you talk with your undivided attention is one of the best ways you can inspire them and show your support. I had to learn this the hard way. After being married three times, I finally got it! Some men pride themselves on being able to watch television, read a magazine, and listen to their wives all at the same time. That is an admirable trait, but it is *not* quality time and sends the message that the wife is not that important.

Instead, I learned to turn off the TV, lay the magazine down, look into my wife's eyes, and interact. Twenty minutes of undivided attention will do wonders in your relationship! Men, if you really want to impress your wife, the next time she walks into the room while you are watching a sporting event, put the television on mute and don't take your eyes off her as long as she's in the room. If she engages you in conversation, turn the TV off and give her your undivided attention. You will score a slam dunk and, after she quits asking you if you're feeling okay, she will be inspired to give you her full attention in return!

Full Tank attention focuses on engaging the present moment and bringing your complete attention to the people and priorities you value most. Many times, once you have identified your life's purpose and passion, your attention will automatically be drawn to matters related to your dreams. It's like when you're shopping for a new car and decide you want a red convertible— all of a sudden you notice every convertible, especially red ones, that pass you on the highway. Once again, your subconscious is magnetically attuned to what you care about and what you're interested in.

An important way to align your subconscious and to direct your attention toward your goals is through vision. What you repeatedly see and "breathe in" is what will inspire you. So make sure your sights are set on the catalysts of your own success.

Full Tank vision mapping

Nothing inspires you like a picture or visual. We don't think in words or sentences; we reflect in pictures and images, memories and mental movies. In 1993, a nine-year-old girl was asked by her teacher to make a vision board. She pinned a photo of the singer Selena holding her Grammy Award. That little girl grew up to become an international superstar, a pop singer named Katy Perry.

It was 1999 after failed marriage number two when a thirty-five-year-old man sat in his tiny studio bedroom and wrote six impossible things he wanted to pursue: (1) recording a gold and platinum music record, (2) traveling the world on music tours, (3) appearing on national TV shows, (4) becoming a pilot and flying his own planes, (5) becoming a motivational speaker for the NBA, and (6) finding the perfect woman for him and his children. All six were achieved by 2009. That man's name is Ben Tankard!

BENspiration

You will *never* leave where you are until you *see* and *decide* where you'd rather be!

A vital component to your success is to surround yourself with what can be, not just what is. That's the power of the Full Tank Life vision. Remember, you don't see *with* your eyes; you see *through* your eyes. As I explained in chapter 4, you have to train your mind and give it a GPS or map of where you want your life to go. Otherwise, you will just follow the status quo of whatever is around you. You will live your life by default instead of by deliberation toward your Destiny.

One of the best tools for harnessing this power is a Full Tank Life vision map. A vision map adds clarity to your dreams and desires. It helps you concentrate and focus on your life goals. Scripture tells us, "Where there is no vision, the people perish" (Prov. 29:18 kjv). Let me give you the Full Tank version of this verse: without inspiration, you will die! Your imagination and the dreams you envision are what sustain you, especially when the going gets tough. They take you from where you are to where you long to be.

Back in Genesis, God told Abraham, "Look up at the sky and count the stars—if indeed you can count them. . . . So shall your offspring be" (Gen. 15:5). He later told Abraham to look at the grains of sand because they also represented the number of his future descendants. God wanted Abraham to have a picture of it in his mind. He gave him clear metaphoric images of his future.

And notice the way God did this. Abraham lived in the desert. What was he surrounded by all night long? Stars. What was he surrounded by all day long? Sand. God knew it wasn't enough for Abraham to hear about his future; he also needed to see where he was headed. He was literally surrounded by God's vision for Abraham's future. Ultimately, he became what he beheld.

When you create your vision with a vision map, a vision book, or even an app on your smartphone, you are seeing yourself the way you want to be. I have been using vision maps for years as a tool to apply my faith, and they have helped to keep me in a state of continual progression.

If you do nothing else as a result of reading this chapter, do this one exercise of creating some kind of vision map for yourself. It may consist of a collage of pictures and images depicting your dreams. It can range from places you want to go, things you want to have, aspirations you want to achieve, and your deepest desires in fulfilling your personal life goals. It's not that the map itself causes your dreams to magically appear; it's what the realization and clarity of your dreams does to *you* that makes it work!

I have experienced the fulfillment of a wide range of dreams (and even personal desires) in my life by consistently having my dreams clearly visible before me. If your life hasn't progressed like you've wanted in the past few years, then perhaps you need vision (and a clear one at that).

What's in front of you is far more important than what's behind you. Sure, you learn from your past. Yes, you turn your messes into a message to help others. But you shouldn't spend more time reliving, rehearsing, or remembering the past when God has so much for you to accomplish in your future.

Paul said, "Brothers and sisters, I do not consider myself yet to have taken hold of it. But one thing I do: Forgetting what is behind and straining toward what is ahead, I press on toward the goal to win the prize for which God has called me heavenward in Christ Jesus" (Phil. 3:13–14). This principle should be applied to every area of our lives. Reach for those things that are ahead! In order to reach for them, you have to be clear on what those things are. So, before you start cutting and pasting away, put a demand on your faith to dream bigger and get clear on what you need to pursue for your Full Tank Life.

BENspiration

"You can't wait for inspiration. You have to go after it with a club."

—*Jack London*

Great Nextpectations

When I was playing basketball, I learned the crucial power of anticipation and expectation. Basketball is a fast-paced game. You have to be ready to execute a play downcourt as soon as the ball's back in your team's possession. You need a sense of timing to think ahead and envision your route and the basket you're about to score.

As a kind of shorthand for this combination of anticipation and expectation, I coined the term *nextpectation*. I would often yell out, "Next down!" or "I got next!" as a way to let my team-mates know my head was in the game and I was fully engaged. I was ready and united with them in the pursuit of victory play by play, shot by shot.

Nextpectations have also been instrumental (no pun intended!) in my concert performances. A lady once came up to me after one of my concerts and said, "Ben, I enjoyed your music so much tonight, but I enjoyed the things you said between the

songs even more." When I asked her why, she replied, "Hmm...
I think you speak to the child in me and you make life seem so
fun. You make me remember what it is like to dream big and not
have any limitations to my imagination."

Smiling from ear to ear, I thanked her and told her how much
her words meant to me. I was also smiling because of the irony of
her words. In another concert a lady had approached me after-
ward and said, "I wish you would do more music and less talking. You're very funny and inspiring, but I didn't come to your
concert for a stand-up routine or motivational speech." It only
goes to show not everyone is going to be on your side and enjoy
what you offer, but that's okay. You have to customize the way
you're called to create, which is often the way that you yourself
receive inspiration.

Creating a performance event that's identical to one that I
would thoroughly enjoy is what inspires me in my concerts. I am
a heart-driven person, and it's very hard for me to speak without
some sort of positive, motivational message slipping out, especially in the area of dreams. These little nuggets remind me of
the nextpectations from my days on the b-ball court.

In other words, I like to motivate people to enjoy the present
and look forward to what's next. And I believe it is wasted time
to reflect, wonder, and daydream merely on what is possible.
What is possible does not require deep reflection—only action.
Dreams and imagination should be fueled by what seems impossible. Just assume that there will be challenges you don't anticipate and obstacles you can't see your way through. But commit
to persevering and never letting anything steal your vision.

When fulfilling your dream appears impossible, step back

and try to get a different perspective or look at what's blocking you from another angle. Notice, too, that the word *impossible* separates into another pair of words: *I'm* plus *possible*. So the only thing separating *impossible* from *I'm possible* is space (and an apostrophe!). Scientists tell us vacant spaces still contain millions of molecules in constant motion; therefore, nothing is ever truly empty. Space has substance and motion even if you can't see it. So you could say the only thing separating *I'm possible* from *impossible* is your patience toward time and your perception of movement.

One Day Island

You're not dreaming big enough if all your dreams can be charted into five easy steps. Possibilities don't require you to draw on your resources and innovative abilities. Attainable goals rarely require you to step out in faith. Similarly, dreams that seem easily within reach rarely inspire you or motivate you to take action. Anything that's possible only causes you to delay and defer your action to another time.

Many people live in a conditional mindset I like to call "One Day Island" or "One Day I'll..." It occurred to me many years ago as I was watching syndicated reruns of the old *Gilligan's Island* show. Gilligan and the Skipper and the other castaways were always talking about what they would do once they were rescued from their deserted island. But in the meantime, their lives were all put on hold as the days, weeks, months, and years ticked away.

Their situation as castaways struck me as the perfect metaphor for people I knew who spent their entire lives stranded in a mindset of conditional thinking. Some would say, "One day, I'll lose weight and get healthy and take care of my body." Others might say, "Yes, I definitely want to be married—one day." Or, "One day, I'll go back to school and finish my degree." "One day, I'll start my own business." "One day, I'll start writing that book I've been thinking about all these years."

When you're on One Day Isle, it's tempting to believe your circumstances are what prevent you from leaving the island and pursuing your dreams. "One day, when I have more money or when the kids are grown or when I find the right job or when I have more time or when I retire..." On and on the excuses accumulate until you begin to feel like you will never get off the island, so why bother trying?

The truth of the matter, though, is that you are the only one responsible for getting off One Day Island because you are the person responsible for marooning yourself there.

Dreaming the impossible gets you a passport off the island; taking action becomes the vehicle for your escape. Your dreams need to be so big that there is no way they are going to happen unless you live by faith.

Flint and Steel

Take control of rescuing your dreams. Don't get mentally hijacked by doubt. The good thing about dreaming big is that it is *free*. There is something about dreaming and thinking "what if" that will force the "how" and "what next?" to reveal themselves. It will likely take some time, but the time will pass regardless. If you continue to paddle your boat off One Day Island, then one day you will reach the shore of your dreams. But you have to paddle a little bit hour by hour, day by day. It's not too late, but you must start today!

I don't believe the Wright brothers knew their dream of flight would evolve into what aviation is today. You'll recall from chapter 1 the story of how Walt Disney would meet with his idea staff and pitch them new creative ideas that had occurred to him. Whenever the staff said, "Great idea, Walt—we can do it," he would cancel the idea and move on to another idea. However, whenever the staff said, "Impossible, Walt! No one has ever done that before," he knew that was the idea to pursue. I shared this story with you previously to encourage you to dream big and to pursue the impossible. Here I use it to remind you to use conflict and opposition—when people who tell you something can't be done—as opportunities to innovate. Persevering beyond the possible leads you to original ways to actualize your dreams.

Sometimes people quit dreaming because they feel like they're "over the hill," that they wasted too much time and squandered too many opportunities in their younger years. But it's never too late if you still have that dream alive inside you! The very fact that someone feels regret means they still care about whatever it is they wished they had done differently. Don't look back and spend time pining over years past. This only wastes more precious time and expends energy in counterproductive ways. Instead look forward and make good on the present and future you've been given. Don't assume your goal is impossible because you're so far away; simply take the next step in the direction where it's waiting.

Your daily actions, those habits that you do deliberately or allow to occur by default, determine your future. If I spent a couple of days with you, I could determine in that short time if you were moving toward your Full Tank Life. Why? Because your daily routine is what determines your success, not just what you do one time. For instance, it is better to work out thirty minutes a day every day than one time a week for three hours. It is better to invest 5 percent of every paycheck for retirement than to invest your big bonus once a year. The secret to ongoing inspiration is consistency and repetition in the direction of your Destiny!

You will attract what you become. Spending time dreaming, meditating, and praying each day will help you focus. Like flint and steel striking together to spark a fire, these activities will illuminate your path and ignite true, custom-made inspiration for your Full Tank Life. Soon you will have a blazing passion within you, the ongoing fuel of inspiration, and an unquenchable fire of fulfillment!

Your DESTINY Diary

Create an "inspiration resource kit" by pulling together the various quotations, images, people, and events that consistently inspire you. You can use a journal, a photo album, a crate or decorative storage box, a woven basket—whatever works for you! Use it as the repository for anything you encounter that inspires you. You will likely have items and images already that you want to store in it, but the following exercises will help you increase your container for inspirational fuel.

Earlier you made a list of the people you presently know who inspire you. What about people you don't know who inspire you? Who are your heroes from history? Other than Jesus, who inspires you most in the Bible? Why?

Who are the role models you see making a Full Tank difference in our culture today? What about favorite characters from fiction? Make a list of your favorite inspirational people, figures, and characters, and keep it handy for when you need a burst of inspiration.

Go online and visit a few websites for your favorite museums, either ones you've visited in person or ones you've always wanted to experience. Browse their features and exhibits and take note of the images and artists who resonate with your spirit. Choose one artist who inspires you and research more about their life and the kinds of creative work they've accomplished. What is it about this artist that speaks to you and your dream?

CHAPTER 7

NETWORK—The "N" in DESTINY

Who's Flying Your Plane?

Your network determines who's supporting your flight and who's pulling you down!

Several years ago, in my zeal to buy my first plane, I got in a hurry and selected the wrong type of plane for my needs. Maybe it's because, at six foot six, I'm always thinking "bigger is better"! But through buying the wrong plane, I learned a crucial lesson about why it's so important to have the right network—a "safety net–work," as it were—to catch you or, better yet, prevent you from falling altogether.

As I've already shared my love of flying and piloting, it will not come as a surprise that I went shopping for my own plane as soon as I had both motives and money. Being at the top of my field as a gospel jazz artist opened many doors for me to travel extensively for live concerts and performances. Soon the invitations were coming in so fast that I was not able to keep my appointments and dates by driving a tour bus or flying commercial. Therefore, I began to shop for a nice used airplane.

Okay, I confess: the model I selected was *big*! In fact, the Beechcraft Queen Air is the biggest civilian, piston twin-engine plane available. After following up on several that were for sale, I found one that seemed like a bargain. That plane was enormous but now the price was small.

Prior to purchase I began to tell friends and professionals in the aviation arena of my intended acquisition. They were unanimous in their response and advised me not to get that plane. The other pilots and aviation geeks like myself all told me I would regret buying the Beechcraft for good reasons: it was underpowered, had finicky geared engines, and had been discontinued, which made parts scarce. Everyone suggested I get something smaller, more economical, a model that would be easier to maintain by most mechanics.

But noooooo! I had to have the biggest and the oldest, and what seemed at the time to be the most prestigious. And I had to have it right away! To make matters worse, the seller offered buy-here-pay-here credit terms, which made it even easier to exercise my impaired judgment (no bank would finance that model of plane because they didn't consider it worthy collateral). Because I had neither the wisdom to accept my network's counsel nor the patience to wait for a better deal on a different model, I rushed into a purchase that ultimately could have killed me.

You see, every flaw and weakness I'd been warned about in that plane all converged at once. Not long after I made the purchase, that plane blew an engine and I had to make an emergency landing on a makeshift airstrip in an Alabama cornfield—where it sat for two years because no parts were available. It was eventually sold for scrap iron.

Lessons learned: (1) Listen to the people you respect enough to solicit their opinion and trust their judgment; (2) When purchasing an aircraft, hire an independent mechanic and conduct a full pre-purchase inspection. This allows you to see what is going on with the plane history and upkeep. If you don't deal with hairline cracks in that engine casing on the ground, those cracks can get bigger when up in the air under pressure, causing a catastrophe. I was in such a hurry to get my first plane that I skipped the prebuy inspection and took the seller's word that it was a solid craft (despite all the advice I was getting from others who cared about me); (3) After you fail to listen to the people whose counsel you should trust, don't make the same mistake again. In other words, listen next time!

Buying that Beechcraft not only taught me about the importance of prepurchase inspections and not taking a seller's word, but it reinforced the significance of having experts who also have my best interests at heart. We all have blind spots, and this isn't a sign of weakness but merely of being human. Trusting others to cover our blind spots and point out what we cannot see or refuse to see can literally save our lives—not to mention save us time, money, and heartache.

I thought I was flying my newly purchased plane, but in the end it was flying me!

BENspiration

"The quality of your life is the quality of your relationships."

—*Anthony Robbins*

Network = Net Worth

No one can enjoy a Full Tank Life without having their relational engines running at full capacity. Simply put, none of us can achieve our dreams by ourselves. The Full Tank Life requires a dedicated pit crew of people supporting you, believing in you, sustaining you, and cheering you as you cross the finish line.

If you're serious about embracing your Destiny and discovering all the abundant blessings God has for you, then you must be willing to invest in relationships and sustain your investment over the long haul. The right relationships at the right time mean the difference between a smooth flight landing at its destination and a rough flight crashing from the weight of too much baggage.

After all, God created us to work together as a team. Even the book of Genesis in the story of the creation points out this team dynamic: "God said, 'Let Us make man in Our image, according to Our likeness'" (1:26, emphasis mine). Right from the beginning, God reveals Himself as a relational deity, three beings—Father, Son, and Spirit—comprising one God. He makes it clear by using these plural pronouns (*us* and *our*) that creating man was a team effort.

Because we are created in His image, it's only logical that we're intended to live in a similar kind of relational harmony. Ideally, this will be the network we're able to weave together from the various acquaintances, friends, neighbors, coworkers, and family we encounter. Obviously, we will have more than three in our network, and they certainly will not be holy and perfect like our Lord. But the impulse to be a part of something bigger, a community of people who love and support each other as they create together, this is in our DNA.

You were born to network with other people. If you don't learn how to get along and network with others, you will never experience the fullness of life God intended for you. He has placed a little of your victory inside other people, and you must mine for it like a gold prospector, sifting and sorting through the various people along your path.

Many will be like the numerous pebbles and stones you find in a creek bed. But occasionally, you will meet a few who are 24-karat gold—mentors, business partners, fellow dreamers, best friends, and kindred spirits. These will offer you nuggets of invaluable support, fellowship, experience, and wisdom. Considering this metaphor, you can see why I believe your network determines your net worth—not just in financial assets but the value of your life's experiences.

Catch and Release

While networking can be like panning for gold, it can also be like fishing. Often we have to work our nets in order to catch any fish; similarly, we must practice our ability to catch new relationships, understanding that many will be released. A few, however, will nourish us with new ideas and expand our ability to adapt to new challenges. These won't be easy to find, but once you do, you want to make these dynamic, inspiring individuals permanent threads in your network.

Many of the advantages and opportunities encountered in life often come down to who you know. We've all seen friends who get their friends hired at work, or maybe we've bene-fited ourselves when a mentor ends up employing us on their team. I'm not advocating any kind of nepotism or "old boys' network" that favors friends and relatives over stronger candi-dates. But it's undeniable that who we meet and enjoy know-ing often creates a launching pad for other dimensions in our relationships.

Even when we believe in the importance of cultivating our networks, we can sometimes try too hard. If others sense we're only interested in them for what they can do for us and not genuinely interested in who they are, then they will likely be repelled. No one likes to feel used, and you should not scheme and contrive to meet someone just so you can try to acquire them as a customer or pick their brain in their area of expertise. People want to be recognized for more than their abil-ity to grant favors; they want to be appreciated for their unique personality and distinct point of view.

Sometimes you may not be "catching any fish" in your net-work because you're casting your net in the wrong pond. Often in order to fuel your dreams and ignite the Full Tank Life, you must move into deeper waters and you must use more than one net. This lesson emerges from one of my favorite Bible stories—the way Jesus went about forming his own network (see Luke 5:1–11).

Early in his public ministry, Jesus was teaching beside a lake one day. He saw some men fishing not far from shore and also spied two boats nearby. So he asked the fisherman in one of the boats to take him out a ways, probably to give himself some distance from the growing crowds there to hear him teach. Jesus also told the fisherman, whose name was Simon, to pull out into deeper water and cast down his nets (see Luke 5:4).

Simon probably tried to be polite, but he told this newcomer that they had been fishing all night and hadn't caught a thing. After all, they were professional fishermen, so they knew a thing or two about fishing—or at least they thought they did. Nevertheless, Simon agreed to cast again as Jesus instructed, if for no other reason perhaps than to humor this strange teacher.

Even if you don't know the story, you can guess what happened. When he cast out his nets this time, he caught so many fish that the nets broke. Even crazier, they were hauling so many fish on board that their boat began to sink! They had to get the other boat to help them bring in all the fish they caught that day (see Luke 5:7). Simon was so spooked and humbled by this incident that he knew Jesus must be a holy man. But rather than sending the shaken fisherman away, Jesus invited him, along with his companions in the other boat, to be "fishers of men" (Luke 5:10 ESV). Don't you love it—from working the net to the networking!

Two important points jump out at me in this story. First, Simon had only cast out a net (singular) while Christ told him to cast out *nets* (plural). It may seem like a tiny, picky little distinction, but knowing how important details always are in the Bible, I don't believe it's insignificant. Because the disciples had only been casting out the one net, they were not prepared for the bountiful harvest God had planned for them. They had to get the other boat to hold all they caught.

I'm convinced when Jesus tells you to cast out your nets, he has already spoken to the fish to jump in your nets! In other words, he often places your blessings in deep waters and lets them know you're on your way. Therefore, you won't find what you're looking for in shallow waters. And you won't be able to contain all that God wants to give you with a single net. You must head to the deep and bring multiple nets!

Discovering Your DESTINY

On a scale of 1 to 10, how supportive, inspiring, and encouraging is your current network of relationships? Who are the most supportive people in your network? The least? Based on your answers, you may need to think carefully about which relationships you invest your time and energy in.

_____

_____

_____

Make a list of people you wish were in your network—try to come up with at least five names. Dream as big as you want to—the president, Oprah, Beyoncé, or whoever! But try to include at least two people to whom you already have access. Choose one of these two and follow up by inviting them to lunch or coffee.

_____

_____

_____

Write a note of encouragement (not a text or email!) or buy a small gift for someone in your network whom you especially appreciate right now. Tell them how much they mean to you and be specific about the ways you've grown and become a better person because of them. Send it right away!

Bark or Bite

We miss out on God's fullness that He has placed in other people for us when we won't network outside of our comfort zones. In order to harvest the friendships and relationships God has prepared for you, you must move into those deeper waters that are often unfamiliar and even a little scary.

You should practice being loving and kind to everyone you meet because you don't know who God has placed in your path today to bless you. When you're oblivious to the needs of others around you, then they're tempted to respond to you with a similar attitude. If you're arrogant, conceited, and defensive with some sort of chip on your shoulder, not only will you *not* bless those around you, but they won't want to bless you! Even when you aren't sure of others' motives, Jesus told us to treat them like we want to be treated (see Luke 6:31), also known as the Golden Rule.

I've also learned to be consistent in treating others with respect because sometimes they turn out to be angels in disguise. Not literally, but it's been my experience that caring about other people—regardless of their appearance or first impression—pays unexpected dividends. You never know who might be a prince disguised as a pauper!

I was reminded of this recently when I was at the airport, hanging out in my hangar and tinkering on my planes. This is where I often go when I'm "busy" and need to escape from Jewel's honey-do list, better known as her catalog of chores. As is often the case, a pilot friend from a neighboring hangar, John, walked over to shoot the breeze. We were chatting about the weather, flying conditions, plane performance—normal pilot chatter—when out of the blue John said, "Uh, Ben, did you know you have an overbite?"

Whoa! Where did that come from?! I was a little taken aback, but because I knew this guy had a good heart, I was not offended by his question. I just laughed it off and said, "Yep, John, I used to suck my thumb as a kid and my parents were never able to afford braces for us, and I guess when I got grown I never got around to getting them for myself." He smiled and said, "Well, I'm going to help you do something about it now." It turned out that my pilot friend John is also known as Dr. John Philipose of Image Orthodontics with three locations in Murfreesboro, Shelbyville, and Tullahoma, Tennessee!

I had known this guy for a couple of years as a *pilot* but never knew he was the same "Dr. John" with successful orthodontic offices all over the area. Because I knew him as a friend, I did not get offended when he asked me about my overbite. In fact, I am super glad I did not get offended because it turned out that the reason he asked me was because he wanted to *give* me free braces!

Keeping your cool and being nice has its benefits. Had I gotten all bent out of shape and started acting defensive by thinking, "Who does he think he is to ask me about my overbite?" then I would have missed out on a very expensive gift an expert wanted to give me. If I had barked, I would have missed correcting my bite! Now I am cheesing at fifty years old with braces for the first time, and it cost me nothing but kindness.

You never get too old to get better.

Diversify Your Portfolio

Opportunities for building your network are all around you. You are the sum total of your experiences, including each person you encounter and each relationship you cultivate, even for a brief season. A conversation with a stranger as you both wait in line may produce a turning point. The kind gesture of someone you barely know might turn your day around. Opportunities to extend your network abound each and every day.

Each person around you contains a different body of knowledge. Mine their memories so you can learn from the treasure chest of their experiences. It is up to you to "drop your pail in their well" and draw it out. "Where *there is* no counsel, the people fall; But in the multitude of counselors *there is* safety" (Prov. 11:14 NKJV). Think of *safety* here not in terms of playing it safe but more in the sense of creating a strong platform, one that can be both launching pad and safety net.

You may be tempted to connect only with people who are similar to you, ones who make you feel comfortable and accepted. However, these individuals often can't challenge you and stimulate growth in pursuit of your dreams. Getting the perspective of someone from a different culture, background, or season of life can be truly transformative. They will see where you are in ways you cannot see yourself. You may not always like what they have to say, but if they're being honest, then you would be wise to accept their insight and use it for your own improvement.

Yes, diversity in your network is essential to your Full Tank Life. Just consider those who surrounded Jesus: a tax collector, a physician, a fisherman, a prostitute, the rich, the poor, the pious, and the scandalous. Some were similar in that they were also Jewish, born and raised in Israel during Jesus' lifetime. Others were foreigners—Samarians and Canaanites, Romans and Assyrians. Some were very energetic while others were passive. Some were explosive like Peter. Others, like James, were more reserved and logical. Some were skeptical like Thomas while others were more devoted like John.

But Jesus loved and ministered to them all. He accepted people where they were, not forcing them to be someone else just to please him. Most of them quickly realized they could not hide who they were from him if they wanted to—after all, he was the Son of God! Christ looked into their hearts and knew them better than they knew themselves.

He also treated each of them with respect and humility. Following his example, I encourage you to be willing to listen to others and assume they have something to teach you. Everyone sees through different eyes. They feel with different hearts. They hear through different ears. Someone knows something that you should know. You will not discover it until you take the time to stop, listen, and hear them out. One piece of information can turn a failure into a success. Diversify your relational portfolio so that you have a vast array of different kinds of wealth.

BENspiration

Full Tankers treasure other people because they assume others always have something to teach them.

Mine Your Mentor

Perhaps the quickest way to strengthen your network is by choosing strong mentors, people who have already experienced success and failures in the areas you aspire to explore. Every relationship can teach you something, but mentors offer a graduate degree in the art of Full Tank living. A mentor is a trusted teacher willing to transfer information to you. Mentorship is gleaning wisdom without the season of waiting, sharing success without the suffering.

Finding mentors is usually not as challenging as we expect. It's typically the act of risking that prevents us from pursuing mentors. So many iconic leaders tell me they're surprised by how few people actually ask them for advice or counsel. Don't be afraid to pursue your top-tier mentors first. Consider who has done what you want to do. Who has achieved what you long to accomplish? How can you best interact with these leaders?

Once a relationship is established, no matter how new or tentative it may seem, follow up with your mentor. Examine your motives and be clear about your objectives. You can't receive from the mentor if you are jealous, angry, agitated, or frustrated with them and their success. This kind of comparison mindset only breeds envy and undermines God's ability to gift you with the mentor's wisdom.

I've been blessed to receive so many gifts from a variety of mentors over the years. Currently, my mentors include my spiritual father, Rick Layton, along with Joel Osteen, T. D. Jakes, Les Brown, Magic Johnson, Tyler Perry, and Steve Harvey. And the best mentoring sessions I've experienced took place during one-on-one encounters like dinner meetings, rounds of golf, or flights around the city together. Attending conferences together or pursuing shared hobbies can also be ideal activities.

However, mentorship does not stop where personal contact ends. You can even be mentored by someone you haven't met in person—through their teaching materials like videos, books, blogs, and websites. I have been highly motivated by all of these mentors I listed, but I have met only half of them and don't get to spend a tremendous amount of time with the ones that I do know. But I read their materials regularly. This keeps my tank full and my network strong.

Mentorship Has Its Privileges

In your Full Tank Life things will begin to progress for you and you will find yourself in the company of some high-level personalities. A networking mindset allows you to emulate your mentors and to appropriate the unique privileges and opportunities that emerge from connecting with them. Think of this as access to a kind of elite membership with benefits. Just as an American Express Gold Card allows you to gain access to amenities and global VIP opportunities, mentors afford you the same kind of entrance to excellence.

Use those privileges! Dedicate yourself to seeking out mentors and then do what's necessary to maximize time with them. For example, my wife Jewel and I often attend marriage seminars on vacation and network with powerful young-minded couples who are playful and still in love even after years of marriage. As a result, we've learned from our friends Joel and Victoria Osteen that it's totally okay to disagree as long as you agree to disagree respectfully.

From Bishop T. D. Jakes and his lovely wife Serita, we've learned to share our business vision with our family so that our kids don't have to hate what we do and feel like they're in constant competition for our attention. Our families learn to be part of our trials and triumphs, encouraging us when we struggle and celebrating with us when we achieve our goals. Your children should be included in your dreams so you can serve as an inspirational role model for them.

Jewel and I have also learned so much from many other mentors, especially on how to handle success. And we find that the more successful we become, the more we need additional mentors. We never want to feel like "we've arrived" and can't learn from the dynamic Full Tankers we so admire.

In fact, one of the most important lessons we've learned from our mentors is to make the most of our time with them. You don't want to blow it when you finally have access to your mentors and role models. There's a balance to the art of relating to a mentor. You don't want to be a starstruck fan or devoted student all the time, nor do you want to act so unimpressed and blasé that your mentor wonders why you're there. Seek to be authentic in your admiration and appreciation for them but make it clear you want to learn from them. Most enjoy giving something back to those climbing the ladder behind them and are more than willing to pass along the life lessons they've learned.

Sometimes we can miss a mentorship moment by being too chatty or mentally insisting that our mentor is no different than we are. After all, they put their pants on the same way you put your pants on, right? True, but don't overcompensate and try to level the relational playing field. You're with them to learn and grow, not to compare and compete. I am not by any means suggesting that you become a person that is less than confident in yourself. I'm just saying that you should be watchful and not pushy when you are allowed access to greatness.

Throughout Scripture, the Bible reinforces this idea by reminding you to be careful when you are in someone's presence. It says if you go to a king's house, put a knife to your throat so you do not look like a glutton when you are standing there. "When thou sittest to eat with a ruler, consider diligently what is before thee: And put a knife to thy throat, if thou be a man given to appetite" (Prov. 23:1–2 KJV). Another Scripture says to "Withdraw thy foot from thy neighbour's house; lest he be weary of thee, and so hate thee" (Prov. 25:17 KJV). Basically, these verses remind us of setting necessary boundaries, both to protect ourselves as well as to respect others.

Access is a marvelous gift. It is also a test because the more you are exposed to somebody, the more they see your heart, your flaws, and your mistakes. Can you handle the gift of access to your mentors?

BENspiration

"If your actions inspire others to dream more, learn more, do more, and become more, you are a leader."

—*John Quincy Adams*

Great at Grateful

We should treat our network of friends and associates, including those that are virtual relationships, with the same Full Tank service we give to our loved ones. They deserve the same level of attention and engagement. You never know when customers and clients might become mentors and motivators.

Fans of various people, events, shows, and movies follow their favorites across social media because of the relationship. They want to know what these people are really like and if they share the same passions, interests, and appreciations. As many would-be celebrities have discovered, ultimately you can't fake who you are anymore. Fans crave authenticity and will remain incredibly loyal to those individuals who share their true selves with them.

I'm convinced any success I've achieved is the result of God blessing my efforts to be all that He made me to be and sharing my gifts with the world. After all, it is an honor to have access to these great relationships. I'm even honored that you are reading this book! You did not have to buy it—you could have selected something else. Similarly, there are a hundred other channels to watch, and you don't have to watch my show *Thicker Than Water: The Tankards* on Bravo. And I realize that the more than four million people who have purchased my music could have very well purchased someone else's. So I'm tremendously grateful for the access that you have given me to your heart. I treasure my network and want to make it valuable to you. For me to have access to your life is a gift.

Gratitude and humility are essential to maintaining and growing your network. Appreciation of those with whom you network will make you *unforgettable*. Find ways to express your appreciation. Do it verbally. Speak kind words of appreciation often. When you express your appreciation, do not do it grudgingly as if it is a pain or an effort. You will become unforgettable to every friend in your life. Exude gratitude frequently if not continuously.

Gratitude nourishes yourself and those around you. When somebody is thankful, it restores what you have given . . . and what you have lost. When you make deposits in others and they begin to show their gratitude and thankfulness, it strengthens you. It restores what you have given up. It is a refueling process, so be great at being grateful!

BENspiration
Gratitude makes every network stronger!

Learning to Listen

Over time most of us will discover one or two people who constantly make our tank fuller and our network stronger. For me, it's my wife Jewel who always keeps me going. I can think of no more powerful a connection of teamwork than that of a spouse. The Bible says, "He who finds a wife finds a good thing, and obtains favor from the LORD" (Prov. 18:22 NKJV).

I am indeed favored by the Lord! Jewel is my biggest supporter and fan and keeps me pumped up and encouraged. I would not be anywhere near the man I am today without her. I call her my "kingmaker" because that's how she always makes me feel—like royalty.

Jewel is the reason I wrote this book. She kept bugging me that I was this *New York Times* best-selling author until I finally sat down to write the book! She is constantly encouraging me to expand. I try to do the same for her, being her biggest supporter and cheerleader. And believe me, I learned the importance of this in a marriage relationship the hard way. Let me explain.

Just as having a loving, supportive spouse can make all the difference in the world, dealing with betrayals, constant conflicts, and ongoing arguments can drag you down. One of the true setbacks in life can be divorce. I have experienced it twice in my younger life. Looking back, I believe the primary cause comes down to the fact that I was not willing to be a flexible listener. Instead, during those seasons I was more of a stubborn talker, determined to have everything my way. When my mind was made up, I would even ignore all signs and warnings from mentors. My mother used to say, "A hard head makes a soft behind"—and she was right. Because I quickly learned nothing can spank you like a judge in a divorce courtroom!

I had to push past my failures as a young husband being on the road two hundred dates a year in the music world and missing my children growing up and all their sports events, pageants, and proms. Years later when I met and wanted to marry Jewel, we actually sat down and received premarital counseling and direction from mentors. And this time I listened! I took this proverb to heart: "Hear counsel, and receive instruction, that thou mayest be wise in thy latter end" (19:20 KJV). With life experiences under my belt and wisdom gained by my failures, I developed into a husband who embraces input from his wife rather than a know-it-all.

As a result we have been married sixteen years, and it has been like heaven on earth. We have an awesome blended family of five children, now grown and some with spouses and children of their own. I shared earlier how we ended up stumbling into our hit reality TV show and how this has made us a stronger family. But it all started from me deciding to learn something from every experience, good or bad.

Turn Up the Volume

Realizing I had been an absent father earlier in my life, I vowed to be present in all my children's lives and give them my undivided attention and unconditional love. Similar to learning from my role in my failed marriages, I learned that parenting requires the art of listening. In fact, the longer I live, the more I learn that sometimes what makes a great parent is not being a parent at all, but a friend.

Why? Because friends make better listeners than parents. Parents often get stuck in teacher mode, which is not always what is needed. Friends don't have any judgments or preconceived notions. Friends don't see you as a baby like parents do. A friend's vision of you is not clouded by the memory of all your mistakes since kindergarten. Sometimes children can solve their own problems if they have an opportunity to hear their own voice in the conversation.

I have learned that the seeds of parenting must be watered with the moisture of friendship. My children will not receive wisdom from me if they can't get past my criticism and rejection of them right where they are in any given moment. Recently I had a conversation with my oldest daughter (she's twenty-eight) that ended with her screaming at me, "You are not hearing me!"

She was right. I was so caught up in the disrespect of her volume (I was raised in the South, where yelling at your parents was a prerequisite for funeral arrangements) that I was missing the content of her message. However, when the dust cleared, we became closer than ever because she was saying she wanted to spend more time with me. She wanted me to respect her as a grown woman and simply listen before filtering it through my role as her father always trying to protect her. I was honored that she was willing to push through and make herself heard.

She reminded me that relationships form a complex web of interactions that can either wrap you up like a fly for a spider or launch you like a slingshot to fly higher than you could on your own. As you focus on fueling your Full Tank Life and growing a strong, supportive network, I encourage you to do a relational inventory and see if there's any sediment that needs removing. Cultivating your network is about identifying and eliminating relationships that may be draining you instead of sustaining you. You must focus on the people who support your dreams and pour energy into your heart. This kind of network will launch your dreams and still catch you when you fall!

Your DESTINY Diary

For most people, there's at least one relationship that constantly consumes more energy than it gives back. Yet for whatever reason, we keep these people in our lives and continue to let them siphon fuel out of our Full Tank Lives. Be courageously honest with yourself, and identify the relationship like this in your life. After you've identified this person, someone who's clearly unraveling your network, write a letter to this person describing your feelings and explaining why you are no longer able to invest in your relationship. Once this letter is written, set it aside for a few days and pray about what to do next. You may decide to send the letter, or better yet, have a face-to-face conversation, or to do nothing and wait. But you will feel better just by identifying this energy leak in your network and writing out your feelings.

Choose someone from your network that you want to know better and ask if you can "shadow" them for an entire day. You will likely have to work out the logistics, but if you choose wisely, it will be more than worth it to see this person operate in their strengths in their usual settings. Once they've agreed to your request, talk to them briefly beforehand about how you can minimize disruption while maximizing your time together as a learning opportunity. Most leaders, mentors, and role models will be honored and thrilled to spend a day with you.

Read a book about how to improve the relationships in your network. You can browse online or in your local bookstore, but here are a few classics I encourage you to consider if you're not already familiar with them:

- *The 5 Love Languages* by Dr. Gary Chapman
- *Boundaries* by Dr. Henry Cloud and Dr. John Townsend
- *The Five Dysfunctions of a Team* by Patrick Lencioni
- *Rising Strong* by Brené Brown

CHAPTER 8

YOU—The "Y" in DESTINY

Taking Flight Requires an Angle Adjustment

Stop hijacking your own success—nothing can stop you but
YOU!

While I've certainly shared some very personal stories with you throughout this book, I've saved my most vulnerable confession for last. I'm not ashamed of it, but when I was growing up, I definitely received some strange looks any time others found out about it. Apparently, they didn't expect to see someone like me—a poor, tall, black kid in Florida—in the public library reading Laura Ingalls Wilder's Little House books. Yep, when I was a kid I absolutely devoured those books and considered them some of my favorites!

On the surface, you might not think Laura and I had much in common. After all, she was writing stories based on her family's experience as pioneers in the Midwest during the late nineteenth century. But I loved that in addition to being well-written and very entertaining stories, the books all had a pioneer spirit.

Whether they were planting crops, fighting off bears, enduring blizzards, or putting out wildfires, the Ingalls family knew what it meant to persevere under harsh conditions. They literally had to make their own roads, cutting down trees and creating their own path.

One of the reasons these books made such a vivid impression on me is because we are all pioneers of our own Destiny. While I'm sure I couldn't have articulated this notion as a boy, I knew that the stories of Laura's life stirred something in me. They worked hard and continually created a better life for themselves. They cherished family and loved each other through all kinds of trials and setbacks. Despite all that happened to them, they were never victims. These values resonated with my own family's as well as my desire to pioneer beyond the life I knew at the time.

Much later in life, I discovered this same spirit in the lives of my aviation heroes, the Wright brothers. What set the Wright brothers apart from other early inventors attempting to create flying machines was their focus. While others relied on more powerful engines and different designs for fixed-wing aircraft, Orville and Wilbur Wright realized the importance of a pilot's ability to alter and control the aerodynamics of a plane's wings. They recognized that wings had to be at certain angles in order to catch the wind current during acceleration.

The brothers also saw the need for this angle to be adjusted in order for a craft to take off, remain in the air, and then land. Using a homemade wind tunnel, they experimented with various models at different angles. Ultimately, this led to their creation of a three-axis control, which is still in use on planes today, allowing pilots to steer an aircraft and balance its equilibrium in the air.

If you want to enjoy a Full Tank Life, then having a pioneering spirit is essential. But as we've seen, wanting to fulfill your dreams and actually fulfilling them requires action. Taking risks to discover your Destiny will sometimes result in failures. What you learn from your mistakes and how you implement those lessons will ultimately determine whether you leave the ground. Like the Wright brothers, you too may need to experiment with the angle of your wings, adjusting them to provide maximum control as you climb higher and higher.

BENspiration

"Success is not final, failure is not fatal: it is the courage to continue that counts."

—*Winston Churchill*

Get Out of Your Way

Having a Full Tank Life all comes back to you. There are no magic words or supernatural secrets for living in harmony with your divine Destiny. It's simply a matter of the choices you make as you commit to follow God's path by uncovering the treasure He's placed inside you.

As your mentor, I believe God has given you *favor*. I define that as a power from above to help you accomplish something that you could not do on your own. It's kind of like putting your guardian angel to work for you to protect you, go before you and sniff out danger and guide you around it, and give you insider tips on how to accomplish your dreams and plans. This divinely guided treasure hunt is an ongoing process of discovery. If you feel stuck or caught in a rut, then you may be blocking your own progress, sabotaging your success, or refusing to take necessary risks.

In other words, you may need an angle adjustment.

The good news, though, is that once you get out of your own way, you can become your greatest ally in fulfilling your Destiny. If you're willing to invest what you've been given to fulfill the dream that's been planted in your heart since birth, then your passionate self-confidence becomes your greatest resource. Knowing in your heart what you were born to do can trump any trial or defeat any disappointment. It's all a matter of perspective.

As you may have noticed, everything about the Tankards is big. Big family, big dreams, and sometimes big problems. Despite setbacks and pitfalls, I remain a man of faith and believe in the Full Tank mentality. This means I like to run on all cylinders, at full throttle, all the time. Even though I might be going a short distance, I prefer a Full Tank of gas.

Or think of it this way. Though I rarely drive over seventy miles per hour, it feels good to be in a car that will do 130 miles per hour even if I'm only driving half that fast. Somehow that ride seems better than with the vehicle that only has a top speed of seventy—you know, the kind that starts shaking and whining like it's about to die. In other words, I believe in having more than enough power in order to release more than enough potential.

BENspiration

You only have to be adequate to experience a mediocre life. But a Full Tank Life revs the engine on your best life—every day!

All in the Family

If you've ever seen our show, then you know my family means everything to me. As I think about how each of our children has blossomed, it reveals a great deal about how God has worked in their lives, guiding them to become the best versions of who He made them to be. For example, my eldest daughter, "Queen Brooklyn" as I like to call her, is fresh off another successful hair and fashion expo and expanding her business to different areas. She has come a long way from the "eternal spring breaker" she was years ago and is a great mother to her daughter Diamond. She is even appearing on top shows like *The Millionaire Matchmaker.*

I figured she would live with us in the Tankard Palace until Mr. Right swoops in on the big horse and they ride off into the sunset to get married. *Wrong!* Evidently, Brookie did not get my dream memo. She has decided she and Diamond can move out on their own. Yes, she's a grown woman, old enough to make her own decisions and no doubt do well. When she makes decisions different from the ones I think she should make, I have to respect this, even if I don't like it.

Sometimes, though, it's easy to approve of the choices my kids make. I believe it was a smart move for my son Benji to purchase a home as soon as possible. Now that he's a married man, renting is convenient for a season, but sometimes it is better to invest that same money into purchasing your own home, especially if you know you are going to be settling down in that city.

Even though we agreed with this move, Jewel and I were forced to put our money where our mouth was when Benji and his wife asked us for a loan to help with the purchase. At first we were a little nervous about lending these college credit juveniles $70,000 for their condo, but I have to say they have been very responsible with their agreement. They quickly paid ahead several months on payments and have done a great job keeping their commitment.

Nothing excites parents more than to see their children succeed. Seeing my children pursue their dreams with passion always makes me a proud father. Britney, one of the most independent Tankard offspring, has embarked on a new fitness venture that is helping people in the community get in shape, and I am super proud of her. Her "Princess Boot Camps" are super tough and are designed to pull the Full Tank potential out of all participants.

Cyrene is the spoiled baby of the family, so of course, we anticipated a little drama in her departure for college. Everyone was at the house to see her off as we left to take her to Washington, DC, for school. Right as we were leaving the driveway with the yard full of well-wishers and family, Cyrene had a tearful meltdown in the car! It finally kicked in—she realized she was leaving home. Dropping her off at college was not nearly as emotional because there we became distracted by all the work required to get the dorm ready. After tearful good-byes, we drove back to Tennessee and the reality of our empty nest.

Our son Marcus went to Bible school and became an international missionary who then traveled abroad to assist people in developing countries. Now thirty years old with a family of his own, he's back in the States with his lovely wife Tish. He claims to miss sleeping on the ground and eating bugs in places like the villages of Africa and India where he visited to share the gospel. But I've assured him we have plenty of natives here who need to know the Good News just as much. So what better place to call home than Murfreesboro at Tankard Palace? He has the support of our loving family plus the opportunity to serve at our Destiny Center and minister to our church family there. It's a win-win!

The Tankards are indeed a wacky bunch, but we love each other and we love people. I am very proud of every family member and know that great things are in store for all of us. God has blessed us to travel on this journey together with Full Tanks that pour into one another!

BENspiration
Just be *yourself*—after all, everyone
else is already taken!

Diamond Destiny

Having a Full Tank Life does not necessarily mean you have to have the best of everything and the biggest of everything or all the kids under one roof. It simply means that whatever hand you have been dealt, you commit to doing *your best* with what you have and what you know. You keep a positive attitude in good times and bad times. And finally, you do all the "possibles" and leave all the "impossibles" up to the One who does impossible the best—God!

I suspect God often keeps us where we are on purpose so we can learn the unique lessons from those circumstances and people around us. Many times this does not feel comfortable, provide convenience, or make any sense from our (very limited) viewpoint. This is the essence of faith in action, taking the steps you need to take today, even if you can see how your path will change tomorrow. God asks us to trust Him, but He also wants us to exercise the abilities He has given us.

While we might think life would be easier and we would be happier if He answered every prayer and granted every favor, the truth is we would be miserable. Like spoiled children uncertain of their own talents, we would never discover the unique treasures God has put inside us. Without living from our divine purpose, we can have everything the world has to offer, but we'll still be dissatisfied. Only living within the adventure of faith can we know the contentment of our Creator and the peace that passeth understanding. Remember, diamonds are only formed under incredible heat and pressure!

One of the best examples I know of a "Diamond Destiny" comes from Joseph's story in the Old Testament. You may have heard about this guy—he had the "coat of many colors" and also ended up being the pharaoh's right-hand man down in Egypt. Far from easy, however, his life was marked by trials, tribulations, and tears to rival anything we might face. As the baby of the family, Joseph started off as his father's favorite, which is why old Joe received that fancy coat. But if you know anything about sibling rivalry, especially among brothers, then I don't have to tell you it was downhill from there—at least for many years.

Being jealous and annoyed by Joseph's prophetic dream, which showed them bowing down before him, the brothers initially planned to murder him. But at the last minute, they came up with another plan: bring little brother out of the pit where they had planned to abandon him and instead sell him into slavery to some passing tradesmen headed south. Big difference, right? But at least he was alive.

One incredible irony in this story filled with many emerges here. If Joseph's brothers had not sold him, then he would not have wound up in Egypt, where he happened to interpret the pharaoh's scary dreams correctly, which earned Joe a major promotion. Knowing seven years of plenty were about to be followed by seven years of famine, Joseph planned accordingly as second-in-command. Many years later, as the famine descended and decimated many Hebrews, Joseph's brothers came knocking, basically begging for some wheat to take home.

They didn't recognize their baby brother, so Joseph had some fun messing with them before revealing himself. Eventually, though, their family was reunited but also saved by the preparation Joseph had undertaken. Through no fault of his own, Joseph found himself a slave, a criminal, and an inmate before God raised him up and fulfilled the divine purpose for which He had created Joseph.

Sometimes I wonder what must have been running through Joseph's mind during those various episodes when one dark turn only revealed another. While I'm guessing he must have struggled with fear, doubt, anger, and depression—after all, he was only human—I'm impressed that Joseph kept the faith. Somehow he knew God had bigger plans for him than to die in some hole in the desert or to rot in some Egyptian prison.

Joseph's circumstances made his life look like he was running on empty; however, inside his heart Joseph was cruising with a Full Tank!

BENspiration
The word *impossible* becomes *I'm possible*
when you add the needed space.

Just Imagine

No matter how bleak your circumstances may appear, no matter how trapped you may feel by the consequences of some bad decisions you made earlier in your life, you always have *choices*. One of the greatest choices you have is the decision concerning what your attitude will be today. You may not be able to control many of the big responsibilities and demands on you and your time today. But you can definitely choose how you respond to them. And how you respond to them—how you *act* on them—is not how you *feel* about them.

When you suffer losses or major disappointments, it's only natural to feel the same kind of emotions Joseph must have felt—fear and doubt, powerlessness and anger, resentment and depression. But you don't have to stay there! You cannot control what you feel—but you can control your thoughts about those feelings! And you most certainly control the actions you take. The mistake we often make is allowing how we feel to color how we view our situation.

I am firmly convinced God's greatest gift to His human creations is our imaginations. One of my reasons for believing this comes out of the story of the Tower of Babel. All these very different people—from different cultures, nations, and tribes—got together and believed they could build a tower all the way to heaven. Now, this was long before the concept of a skyscraper or airplanes. And let me just remind you, non-pressurized planes run out of oxygen somewhere around ten thousand to twelve thousand feet off the ground. So somehow, these Babel builders thought they knew how to deal with the hazards of high altitudes.

Because God basically acknowledged that it was possible by thwarting their plans. As you may recall, He gave them all different languages so that they could no longer understand and communicate with one another. As a result, they stalled out and the tower never got off the ground, literally. Apparently, He knew the power of the human mind—especially since He created it!

Now, the conclusion I draw is that these builders, through the power of their imaginations, knew how to pursue the construction of this amazing tower that would connect earth with heaven. Does this mean they would have invented cranes and bulldozers and concrete much sooner? We can't know... but somehow they were close enough to making their vision a reality that God shut it down. He knew if they succeeded then they would view their tower and themselves as idols. God repeatedly makes it clear that He wants His people to have no other gods before Him.

Babel is not my only example. Consider the admonition Jesus gives us about the power of our minds. He said that if we lust after another person in our hearts, we've committed adultery, and if we've hated them then it's the same as murdering them from God's perspective. Those are some mighty powerful thoughts!

If you think about human history, however, from the creation until right now as you read this very sentence, the potential for what we're capable of creating has always existed. When Adam and Eve were in the Garden, inside their DNA was the genesis of the Internet, laptops, cell phones, and satellites. Sounds crazy, doesn't it? But we know they were created in the image of God just as we are. The potential was always there, developing and maturing throughout the generations. Which makes me wonder: What are we on the brink of inventing, discovering, and building to transform our world?

Maybe you and I are not destined to discover the cure for cancer or some new kind of lifesaving machine, but surely God has gifted us with the power of our imaginations for a reason. Using our imaginations, we are able to cast a vision and then work backward, step by step, to make that vision come to life. Why not improve our painful relationships? Why not raise our contentment level? Or restore our finances? It may sound like science fiction, but our ability to see ourselves living a Full Tank Life is the first step. Your miracle begins right this minute—can you see it?

Discovering Your DESTINY

What area of your life are you currently most excited about? Work? Your relationships (network)? Family? Home? Your education? Something else? What's going on in this area that energizes and delights you, filling your tank with more fuel?

_____

_____

_____

What area of your life is presently causing you the most stress? How long has this struggle been going on? Is it temporary or chronic? What have you tried doing to resolve the stress and fix the problem? What do you still need to do?

_____

_____

_____

Knowing you're only human and no one's life will ever be perfect, in which areas of your life do you need to forgive yourself for past mistakes? How can you show compassion and understanding to yourself for what happened in the past? Do you need to talk to others and perhaps ask for their forgiveness, too? Do whatever it takes to remove this burden from your heart so that you have more energy to focus on moving forward in your Full Tank Life.

_____

_____

_____

Expect to Expand

When you can't see it, then you're likely to drain your own tank. Instead of being like Joseph, we end up feeling like Job. Have you ever felt like Job when he said, "My life drags by—day after hopeless day," and "I hate my life. Oh, leave me alone for these few remaining days" (Job 7:6, 16 TLB). I don't want each year you live to be just a repeat of the previous one. Even if the last several months have been really productive, God always expects us to do more, to reach for more, to grow, to expand, and to go beyond previous barriers.

Faith cannot work without action, and no action works without faith. You need both the fuel of faith and the engine of action to make your FTL a reality. Your life will change to the extent that you continue to envision, grow, hope, and dream. When you stop dreaming, when you let go of hope, then you've given up. It's hard for God to bless you when you're looking down, expecting nothing. He wants us looking up at Him and following His direction.

This is how we pursue our Destiny and make it our reality. We're told, "Cast not away therefore your confidence, which hath great recompence of reward. For ye have need of patience, that, after ye have done the will of God, ye might receive the promise.... If any man draw back, my soul shall have no pleasure in him.... We are not of them who draw back unto perdition" (Heb. 10:35–36, 38–39 KJV).

An empty tank mindset avoids challenges and only expends temporary efforts until it's intimidated by the success of others.

The Full Tank mindset, on the other hand, punches through setbacks, falls forward, and remains inspired by the success of others.

As I've stressed, *you* have to *decide* to answer God's calling on your life. It is a deliberate decision. And the decision is all yours. *You* are the only one who can answer it, and *you* are the only person preventing you from answering and embracing that call. As we've discussed, God is calling you to pursue His plan for your life; you just may not be listening or you may be ignoring it. But as you'll recall from chapter 5, you must not let anyone or anything stand in your way:

Don't let your past keep you from answering the call.
Don't let people keep you from answering the call.
Don't let finances keep you from answering the call.
Don't let Satan talk you out of answering the call.
Don't let "busyness" keep you from answering the call.
Don't let insecurity keep you from answering the call.

Your decision to ignore God's plan or to pursue it will affect you forever. If you want to fulfill the very purpose you were born for, you have to prioritize your life. And spending time with God has to be your number one priority. Spending time with the Lord is the very thing that has brought the most healing to my life. It's built my confidence where I was terribly insecure and feeling inferior. It has given me courage to walk away from things that used to have such a hold on me. It has truly changed me from the inside out.

Jesus needed time alone with his Father before he stepped

into the public spotlight. If God's own Son needed to spend time alone with his Father in order to carry out his divine Destiny here on earth, then it should go without saying that you and I need to do the same. Spending time with God is the best way to discover His plan for your life. And you don't have to devote an hour every morning or three hours on your knees in prayer. When you spend even ten uninterrupted minutes each day just to be with the Lord, but you're consistent with those ten minutes, you will hear from God! You will gain insight and direction for your life. Consistency is the key to change.

Expectation is the breeding ground for miracles and divine encounters and favor of God. When you're living with expectations, you will change your environment before it changes you. Expectation eats discouragement for lunch every day! And the key to sustaining your Full Tank expectations is expansion. The Bible says, "Enlarge the place of thy tent, and let them stretch forth the curtains of thine habitations: spare not, lengthen thy cords, and strengthen thy stakes" (Isa. 54:2 KJV).

Expansion is unique and tailored to each individual's life. For some, expansion is launching that new app or finishing that book you've always dreamed of publishing. For others, expansion is a special vacation with your kids or strolling along the beach. Anything that increases your capacity to imagine and dream qualifies as expansion and increases your expectations.

Expansion requires looking past your limiting beliefs about yourself. Easier said than done. If it were easy, all of us would be sailing off into the aforementioned sunset. Relationships help you set new horizons because who knows your limitations better than your own family, friends, and inner circle? Once again, you must surround yourself with a network of supportive, inspiring, energizing, loving people.

Expansion doesn't necessarily have to mean bigger. It may mean deeper. For example, you may want a different house or career change, but you may also want to grow more fully as a person, expanding your ability to forgive and express compassion for another human being. Expansion may be about building a family or deepening your relationships with your loved ones. It's about reaching out past your comfort zone and embracing more of who you are—creating a *vision*!

But what keeps us from expanding and living the vision of our life? The answer is our beliefs. So if you are ready to drop some of your outdated views about yourself and incorporate a little discipline into your schedule, you just might find yourself developing a better life—a better *you*!

You're in the Driver's Seat

Two snakes are slithering down the road, and Snake 1 says to Snake 2, "Are we poisonous?" Snake 2 says, "Of course we are, you idiot—we're snakes! Why would you ask that?" Snake 1 says, "Because I just bit my lip!" The moral is you are the one that determines your life. You can't control others' outdated views of you, but you can control your outdated views of you! It is all inside you. How *you* see something is very important.

As an exercise, look at the ways you limit your ability to create, and then look at the ways you can turn it around and start moving in the direction of your desires. Most of the time, we focus on the negative, what isn't working. With the topic of expansion and vision in mind, focus and get clear about your limiting areas, not to indulge them, but to transform them and move on. Remember, you can't heal what you don't acknowledge. Instead of going round and round with the same issue, have a face-to-face and acknowledge it in order to come up with viable solutions and steps you can take in order to move forward.

Expansion requires deliberate attention to nourish and nurture your dreams. If you want to create more in your life, focus on it. Give it attention. Do something different. Sometimes life is so filled with challenges, we forget about all the good things happening around us. Part of learning how to expand means focusing on what is good in life, not what isn't working. Count your blessings and follow them like breadcrumbs to the next area of abundance in your life.

BENspiration

"Success seems to be connected with action. Successful people keep moving. They make mistakes, but they don't quit."

—*Conrad Hilton*

More Than You Think You Are

Whether it's a superhero movie or a high school football team, the Olympics or a reality show singing competition, we love to root for an underdog. And there's a reason why they hold so much appeal. They give us hope that we can do more, be more, in fact that we are more than we appear on the surface. They inspire us to keep going against all odds and to rethink the way we view ourselves. Underdogs remind us that we're not always who we think we are—we're so much more!

Perhaps nobody in the Bible illustrates this more dramatically than Gideon. In many ways, he's the ultimate underdog—a guy no one expected much from, including himself. His country and culture are in trouble, his family's in trouble, yet Gideon—who just happens to also be the youngest and scrawniest—is the one God chose to be a leader and overthrow the bad guys.

And Gideon definitely had his work cut out for him. The invading tribe who had conquered Israel, the Midianites, included some bad dudes (see Judges 6:1–6). They were worse than *Game of Thrones*, *The Lord of the Rings*, and *Call of Duty* combined! Pillaging and plundering, taking everything edible or valuable, the Midianite marauders had the Israelites running and hiding for their very lives. And then when that week's raid seemed over, they would come out of hiding only to discover their fields and farms reduced to dust.

The Israelites had to have been constantly afraid and wondering when the next attack would occur. But God heard their prayers and was ready to help them by raising up a leader to defeat their adversaries. That's where our underdog Gideon comes in:

The angel of the LORD came and sat down under the oak in Ophrah that belonged to Joash the Abiezrite, where his son Gideon was threshing wheat in a winepress to keep it from the Midianites. When the angel of the LORD appeared to Gideon, he said, "The LORD is with you, mighty warrior."

"Pardon me, my lord," Gideon replied, "but if the LORD is with us, why has all this happened to us? Where are all his wonders that our ancestors told us about when they said, 'Did not the LORD bring us up out of Egypt?' But now the LORD has abandoned us and put us into the hand of Midian."

Judges 6:11–13

Obviously, there are two different perspectives intersecting here. God finally sends his angel to Gideon with a message of hope about how to defend and restore His people. But instead of being excited, hopeful, or even curious, Gideon reveals some stinkin' thinkin' about his current circumstances. Basically, he says, "Uh, are you talking to me? Really, Mr. Angel? God is here with us? If that's true, then why am I hiding out threshing wheat—women's work—without even having the proper tools? I don't see the Red Sea parting for us anytime soon."

The details of the scene emphatically reveal the extent of national distress the Israelites were experiencing. Gideon was threshing wheat in a winepress, which could only process a small amount of grain at a time. He was actually outside under a tree, not in a threshing room or mill. In his culture what he was doing usually fell to the women in the family while the men were out farming, hunting, and fighting. But here sits Gideon when the angel shows up and tells him that he's a "mighty warrior."

Maybe you've felt this way, too. Either you had a sense of God calling you to a task for which you felt poorly prepared or else you found yourself in a circumstance where it felt impossible to overcome adversity.

However, God is bigger than our lack of experience, insecurities, and fears. Just because we think something seems true, probable, or accurate does not mean it's that way from God's point of view. Jesus said, "With man this is impossible, but with God all things are possible" (Matt. 19:26). We often allow our thoughts to label our perception of our identities as well as our circumstances. But God loves to inject His miraculous power into our midst and remind us of what's really true: We're not what we think. We are who He says we are, and with Him as our loving Father, all things are possible—even things we can't imagine.

BENspiration

The word *stressed* spelled backward is *desserts*—it's all in the way you look at it!

Make Up Your Mind

The human mind is a funny thing. Our brains contain such power and complexity, facilitating the way our bodies operate while processing data from our surroundings. Drawing on our intelligence, imagination, and emotions, our minds can change our attitude and demeanor in mere seconds. We can go from total fear when we look up and see a child in danger to absolute relief when the car brakes in time to avoid hitting him, followed by a flood of joy and gratitude that this precious life wasn't harmed.

Over the course of our lives, as our base of knowledge and basis of comparison among our life experiences increases, we begin to think we have certain things figured out. Like I said, growing up, I had a tough time. The events and experiences of my upbringing strongly influenced how I perceived myself, others, and life in general. As a result, I came to trust the way I saw myself as the way I must be. Or, as the Bible explains, "For as he thinks in his heart, so *is* he" (Prov. 23:7 NKJV).

When I think I'm a failure, I feel like a failure. When I think I'm unprepared and unable to do something, that image of myself becomes my focus. Some people are hypochondriacs, so when they think something is wrong in their body because of a weird pain, they start freaking out and assume the absolute worst must be true. The scratch becomes a snakebite, the blister becomes a tumor, and a fever must be a symptom of a terminal disease. You know what I'm talking about—if you're like me, you've probably been guilty of it a time or two!

Many of us have thoughts that are very real in our heads, but they're not the reality of our lives. In your mind you assume that just because your pulse is pounding you're having a heart attack, but the reality is that your heart is responding to the stress and adrenaline in your body. But the more you worry about the worst, the more you start to sweat and worry and become gripped by fear. Because your mind and body were designed to work together, they have a strong connection. So when your mind sends out the red-alert alarm that something's wrong, your body responds accordingly, which only sustains the alarm signals to your brain. Our thoughts are so powerful!

Our thoughts, perceptions, assumptions, and expectations often work the same way in our lives. We think something's true and only notice details and evidence supporting what we already tend to believe. Many of us hold on to a label because of wrong or negative thinking. We label ourselves a failure because we think we are a failure. We label ourselves worthless because we think we are worthless. We think God can't use us, so we don't surrender ourselves to Him. We think our family is hopeless, so we then operate with that mindset. And such thoughts hinder us from reaching our God-given potential.

The mind obsessed by weakness cannot produce the strength we need. The mind of a broken person cannot produce the life of a healthy person. The mind of defeat cannot produce a life of victory. The mind of fear will not produce a life of faith. We will never go beyond the barriers in our own mind. If we think we can't do something, we never will. If we are defeated in our minds, we have already lost the battle; if you don't think your dreams will come to pass, they never will. If you don't think you can overcome an addiction, situation, or lifestyle, you never will.

The battle is won or lost in between your two ears.

BENspiration

Embracing your Destiny requires you to redefine yourself as God sees you—with the "eyes of faith"—as things will be, not as they are.

Courage Is Overrated

From my experience, the essence of courage is not thinking about what it takes to do something but just doing it! Courage grows over time, so do it scared now and develop guts later on. Remember, when expanding your life, courage and risk are key ingredients. You have to be willing to risk losing the old, familiar part of you that isn't working or that is limiting your life. This is where it can get tricky. Because even though you say you want to change, you also may feel very attached and comfortable with this part of your life. Expanding means eliminating what is no longer useful and productive.

So as we reach the end of our journey together, let me encourage you to ground who you are in practicality but be willing to expand into the vision of who you are. The Full Tank Life is self-defined. Only *you* know what will make you happy and fulfilled. My job has been to motivate you through proven steps that will put you on the fast track to achieving your own. You have the purpose, passion, and power to accomplish all the dreams God has planted in your heart. The time is now. Your tank is full. Your engine is revving.

You can do it!

BENspiration
Vision without *action* is fantasy and action
without *vision* is chaos.

Your DESTINY Diary

How have you sabotaged your own success in the past? What are the emotional triggers that often send you moving backward instead of forward? Create a plan of response to help you deal with these unexpected moments when you feel ashamed, afraid, angry, jealous, or unworthy of the dreams God has given you to pursue. Be sure you include prayer as key to your action plan—because your spiritual enemy knows your weaknesses and will try to use them against you every time. But God has already won the victory, so ask Him for protection!

_____

_____

_____

What's the single biggest change you've made since you started reading this book? How has it improved your life and brought you closer to your dreams? What's the next logical step you can take to maximize this positive change and create Full Tank momentum?

_____

_____

_____

In your own words, not mine or anyone else's, provide your own personal definition of a Full Tank Life. What does it look like, smell like, taste like, feel like in the context of who

you are, how God has gifted you, and your present circumstances? What elements are beyond your ability to change
or control? Which elements can you influence or impact?
And finally, which ones are solely up to you?

_____

_____

_____

DESTINY—All Systems Are Go!

A Full Tank for a Lifelong Journey

How you finish depends on starting right now.

In previous chapters we've explored many different dimensions to get you motivated to dream, plan, and execute. However, be forewarned that you *do* have an enemy out there, and just because you decided to have a Full Tank Life does not mean that he will give up on his attempt to shipwreck your faith-fueled journey. He will try to derail your efforts and drain your Full Tank at every turn.

There will be days you won't want to get out of bed, times when you cannot see any positives, and moments when you feel like quitting the human race. Yet these are the times when we must keep going, just one more step. The Bible confirms the need to persevere: "Here on earth you will have many trials and sorrows. But take heart, because I have overcome the world" (John 16:33 NLT). Maybe it's my Full Tank translation, but what I hear God telling us is clear: "Do not become weary. Your present circumstances will change. You will rebuild. You will grow if you refuse to stay down. It may take a little time, but you will win again."

Reserve Fuel Tanks

You must beware of certain mind traps that may occur immediately after a temporary setback in your life. When people let you down and events don't go the way you hoped, it's tempting to view these setbacks as permanent limitations. But if you view setbacks as setups for your next opportunity to prevail, then those obstacles crumble and become nothing more than dust beneath your feet. Here are some of the most likely traps that can sabotage your progress along with some "reserve fuel tanks" to fill you back up:

Denial

When you ignore or minimize what's happened in your life—both your failures as well as your accomplishments—then you cut yourself off from your soul. Usually, denial works as a temporary emotional coping mechanism to help us get through something unbearable. But as a chronic way of confronting your life, denial never works. It's like driving around on four spare tires! A spare is intended to get you by when you have a flat, not be the standard to replace all four tires.

Problems do not go away just because we refuse to look them in the eye. It's dangerous to pretend everything will all just work out in the end. Because the longer you keep your head in the sand, the longer you prevent yourself from finding solutions and moving on.

Break free of denial by accepting the truth and getting help to resolve your issues. This is where your network can play a huge role in supporting, sustaining, and stabilizing you. The people who care about you will tell you the truth and not judge you for struggling. They will remind you of the bigger picture, not just the immediate issue in your field of vision. They will allow you to lean on them as you catch your breath and regroup before continuing on your journey.

Powerlessness

Powerlessness tends to hijack our progress because it tilts us toward the "V" word: *victim.* When you feel like you have no options and no control, then it's hard not to feel like a victim. This mindset leads to ongoing, unresolved anger, which is ultimately destructive and can undermine what we've worked so hard to attain.

From my experience confronting situations that appear beyond my control, anger often works hand in hand with fear to create a powerful poison. And fear is often tied to what feels uncertain and beyond our control. What we do not understand, we fear. What we fear, we fight. What we fight, we destroy. When this toxic mixture gets in your tank, it doesn't take long to clog your engine. It progresses from a temporary feeling about one situation to a consistent attitude toward all situations. We see it emerge when we start speaking in absolutes:

"You *never* wanted me to do this."

"You *always* act this way when there's a problem."

"This happens *every* time when you don't get your way."

"It's no use—the situation is totally *hopeless*."

Such a rigid stance does nothing to help you reclaim your power and break free of this psychological paralysis. In order to stop feeling powerless, start by recognizing your choices. And you *always* have choices! You may not like them—and you don't have to like them—but you need to identify them and then deliberately decide which way you're going to go. In other words, make a plan and then start working the plan. I know it sounds simple, and most situations making us feel powerless are almost always (I said "almost") complicated. But list your options, make your choice, and just identify the next step to take.

Depression

Like coming down with the flu, getting depressed never happens at a convenient time—mostly because there's not one. These painful, negative, sad feelings seep into your system at the most inappropriate times; it may occur around holidays, birthdays, anniversaries, and special occasions, or it can strike at seemingly random, uneventful moments such as eating dinner with friends or waking up at two a.m. only to discover you can't go back to sleep.

Lord knows I'm no psychologist, but from my own experiences, depression is usually the result of introspection. When I watched my NBA career crash before my eyes, I could think of nothing else for weeks and weeks. I replayed the moment of my injury over and over again, wondering how I could change the outcome and recover my precious dream of pro stardom. But no matter how long or how intently I brooded, I couldn't change what had already happened.

The cure is to discipline our thoughts toward a goal in our future or to concentrate on helping *someone else* achieve a worthy goal. Now, I know there are clinical kinds of depression and medical factors that require professional help and even medications. But the kind of depression that comes with pursuing your Destiny is usually temporary and triggered by a painful loss or unexpected disappointment. This kind of depression requires action—not reaction. Use your memories for *ministering* to others, not self-destructive meditation on what might have been! It is impossible to think wrong *and* feel good at the same time.

Drama

No, I'm not talking about your favorite soap or the tear-jerker movies you love to cry over. This kind of mental trap is the drama that comes from the urgency inflicted by other people's issues. You know what I'm talking about: your passive-aggressive boss who drives you crazy with her mixed messages, friends who force you to take sides when they're fighting, and relatives who want to pull you in to fixing their problems.

Don't get me wrong—I'm all for helping others and supporting them in healthy, constructive, and encouraging ways. But people who are into drama don't want anything more than your time and attention. They don't want help or solutions as much as they want to be the center of attention and have their fifteen minutes in the spotlight—on a daily basis!

Boundaries, including the confident use of *no*, are the remedy for eliminating these distracting and destructive dramas from your life. Staying focused on your own dreams and Destiny requires you to set limits and to walk away from certain situations and certain people in your life. Don't become a walk-on player in someone else's drama. Be the star of your own story and keep your spotlight on your future.

Stay away from these mental traps because they will keep you running on empty most of the time. The Bible says faith comes by hearing truth (see Rom. 10:17), so don't forget to hit reset every morning and push play on your passion and purpose. While I mean this as a metaphor, I also mean it literally. Download motivation messages, sermons, and speeches on your phone or digital device and play one every time you're getting dressed or undressed. Even when you hear the same message over and over again, it can still have power to motivate you if it's based on God's Word.

Remember this: Whatever you hear, you think...whatever you think, you eventually say...whatever you say, you eventually do. Whatever you focus on will grow until it becomes bigger and fills your life. If you focus on problems, then they will get bigger and consume you. If you focus on solutions, then your peace and joy will grow as you resolve your problems.

BENspiration

"Perseverance is not a long race; it is many short races one after the other."

—*Walter Elliot*

Dreamers' Hall of Fame

Whenever I get discouraged or start doubting myself, I like to review my "Dreamers' Hall of Fame." These are the stories of individuals who have overcome countless obstacles to achieve their dreams and fulfill their God-given Destiny. Reminding myself that they too faced impossible odds and wrestled with fears and doubts always inspires me to keep going for one more day. If you think your dreams are too big to believe, if you believe you're up against something you can't overcome, then check out these dreamers who went through the same kind of challenges before fulfilling their Destiny. Here are a few of my favorite exhibits in my Full Tank Dreamers' Hall of Fame:

Thomas Edison's teachers said he was too stupid to learn. He reportedly created over five hundred light bulbs before he built one that worked. In addition to electric lighting, he went on to invent a two-way telegraph, a carbon telephone microphone, and a video recorder of moving pictures. He held over a thousand patents, individually and jointly, for his numerous amazing inventions.

Colonel Harland Sanders knocked on over a thousand doors with his special fried chicken recipe before restaurant owners finally gave him a shot. Part of the problem for many prospective backers was Sanders's age—he was sixty-five at the time! Colonel Sanders not only went on to create the successful Kentucky Fried Chicken franchise, but he was one of the first visionaries to extend his "finger lickin' good" fast-food chain internationally.

By the mid-1960s KFC had opened its restaurants in Canada, Mexico, Great Britain, and Jamaica.

Academy Award–winning director Steven Spielberg was rejected from the University of Southern California's prestigious film program three times, and then after he was accepted, he dropped out! Spielberg, you may recall, is responsible for such iconic films as *Jaws*, *Close Encounters of the Third Kind*, *E.T.*, *Indiana Jones*, *The Color Purple*, *Schindler's List*, and *Saving Private Ryan*, just to name a few!

Soichiro Honda was fired from his engineering job at Toyota headquarters in Japan. He then began making motorcycles, and his first bike was called the Model D—and, yes, the "D" stands for dream! Within a very short time, the Honda Motor Company produced more motorcycles than anyone in the world. Its creator not only became a wealthy man, but he never forgot "the power of dreams"—which became his company's slogan.

Walt Disney was fired by a newspaper editor because he lacked imagination. Can you believe that? Today most of our childhoods would not be the same without the wonderful world of Walt's vivid imagination come to life. Mickey and Minnie, theme parks, Pixar. And today the Walt Disney Company also owns the ABC television network and George Lucas's *Star Wars* franchise. Not bad for someone lacking in imagination!

Albert Einstein did not speak until he was four years old, and he could not read until age seven. As a result of his slow development, he was labeled "mentally handicapped"! Turns out, he just had a different way of thinking—the kind that leads to a Nobel Prize in Physics!

Theodor Geisel, better known by his pen name "Dr. Seuss," was turned down by twenty-seven publishers before one agreed to give his children's book a shot. His books went on to be translated into twenty languages and sell over six hundred million copies worldwide. That's a lot of cats in that hat!

As a kid growing up in Georgia, Truett Cathy had a paper route and saved as much money as he could. Using his savings, as a young adult he and his two brothers opened a tiny twenty-four-hour café, the "Dwarf House," in the rural outskirts of Atlanta, which turned profits from the first week. Three years later, Cathy's two brothers and business partners were killed in a car accident. He kept the restaurant going, but within a few years it burned down—and it wasn't insured. As if his Job-like circumstances weren't already bad enough, Cathy discovered a tumor in his colon requiring surgery and months of recovery. Instead of rebuilding his business, he was forced to remain in bed.

Depressed and discouraged, Cathy had a dream during this period of recuperation. His dream involved a special kind of chicken sandwich, one seasoned differently than any other, served simply on a bun with only a pickle. Yep, you and I enjoy these same "dream sandwiches" today at Chick-fil-A!

Your story is just as inspiring as these Hall of Famers! Just don't give up. Keep going. And find a way to push through every obstacle life throws at you—even when you have to go through the roof!

Discovering Your DESTINY

Whose name in the Dreamers' Hall of Fame, and the obstacles they had to overcome, surprises you the most? Why? What can you learn from their example to apply to your own life? What did they learn from their setbacks that you can use to overcome your own?

_____

_____

_____

Review the people you listed in chapter 6 as well as those in your network. Which of these individuals belongs in your own Dreamers' Hall of Fame? Why? What criteria would you use for your own special list of the all-time greatest dreamers?

_____

_____

_____

Write out your own entry for membership in the Dreamers' Hall of Fame by starting with your greatest future achievement and then working backward to where you are now and the obstacles you will overcome to get there.

_____

_____

_____

Hole in the Roof

Yes, life is filled with the unexpected, the uninvited, and the unbelievable. The key is to keep your dreams alive so you can keep running on a Full Tank, enjoying the process even when you must overcome adversity. This requires staying in motion and not letting temporary roadblocks turn into permanent dead ends.

As I've shared with you throughout these pages, we can't sit around and *wish* things would change—we've got to *do* something! Where there's a will, there's a way to find your way! One of my favorite stories of "finding a way" involves the determination some friends had to help one of their own recover his health.

In Luke 5, we read the story of the four men taking their sick friend to see Jesus for healing. The place was packed and there was no room for them to get in. So they went the extra mile. They didn't conclude that there was nothing they could do and turn around and go home. They didn't tell their friend, "Man, we tried—I'm so sorry..."

No, they were proactive! They found a way to get their buddy in that house in front of the Master. They made a way where there was none. "When they could not find a way to do this because of the crowd, they went up on the roof and lowered him on his mat through the tiles into the middle of the crowd, right in front of Jesus. When Jesus saw their faith, he said, 'Friend, your sins are forgiven'" (Luke 5:19–20).

Notice it says, "When Jesus *saw* their faith." How can you see faith? By seeing it in *action*. I'm thinking the Lord was at least impressed by their tenacity and resourcefulness. And He gave them what they were after. Jesus healed him.

Would you have been willing to cut a hole in the roof and lower your sick friend down right in front of Jesus? Or would you have been too self-conscious, too polite, too afraid of what other people would think? When faced with the impossible, we have to find a way to cut a hole in the roof of our obstacles and bring them before the Lord. He has given us talents, intelligence, and imagination to face every problem we encounter.

Like these roof-cutters, we must be proactive in the same way and persevere until the temporary no in our life becomes a permanent yes. This means we have to *do* something—even if we're not sure if it's the best thing. We can have all the faith in the world, but if we don't take a step and act on it, then it doesn't accomplish anything. "Faith apart from works is useless" (James 2:20 ESV).

So what do you need to do? What's your next step after reading this book to put your faith in action and embrace your Destiny? I told you at the beginning of our journey together that your time is right now. So do it. Enroll in that class. Call the travel agent. Book the trip. Meet with the bank. Update the resume. Form the corporation. Launch the business. Write the book. Meet with the Realtor. Join the gym. Save the money. Propose to the one you love. Record the CD. Volunteer at the shelter. Give the interview. Audition for the part.

Nothing happens until you take action.

SO DO IT!

BENspiration

Nothing will change until you decide that you will change it and take action! Change begins inside your mind and then acts outside your body.

Don't Forget to Remember

We have talked a lot about how to define and develop your Full Tank Life, but I want to share how to keep your life's tank full once you experience it. As we have seen, when you're developing your life goals, you have to determine the what, where, when, and who, and then allow God to reveal the how. But once you're up and flying off the ground, you still have to remember where you came from. You can't suddenly develop a case of amnesia about how you got where you are!

Or perhaps even worse is when you begin rewriting your past to fit in with your new success. We see this happen with celebrities and political candidates frequently. Their public persona and lifestyle look a certain way, and the stories they tell about growing up and stepping into the spotlight reflect this same attitude, their brand. But then it comes out that they've embellished their story, or even outright lied about it. Their self-made success pulling themselves up by their bootstraps collapses when it's clear their family was wealthy to begin with. With others, their warm, conservative morality is at the core of their brand until their past lovers and drug dealers share evidence to the contrary.

This problem is not a new one caused by social media and the Internet. It's as old as human nature and one we see frequently in the Bible. In fact, the entire Old Testament is filled with stories of how the people of Israel were constantly up and down in their roller-coaster relationship with God. They were enslaved, needy, and desperate in Egypt, so God rescued them and led them to the Promised Land. But even after such a dramatic advancement, the Hebrew people tended to suffer from spiritual amnesia. So God had to keep reminding them, like He does here:

> When you have eaten and are satisfied, praise the LORD your God for the good land he has given you. Be careful that you do not forget the LORD your God, failing to observe his commands, his laws and his decrees that I am giving you this day. Otherwise, when you eat and are satisfied, when you build fine houses and settle down, and when your herds and flocks grow large and your silver and gold increase and all you have is multiplied, then your heart will become proud and you will forget the LORD your God, who brought you out of Egypt, out of the land of slavery. He led you through the vast and dreadful wilderness, that thirsty and waterless land, with its venomous snakes and scorpions. He brought you water out of hard rock. He gave you manna to eat in the wilderness, something your ancestors had never known, to humble and test you so that in the end it might go well with you. You may say to yourself,

"My power and the strength of my hands have produced this wealth for me." But remember the LORD your God, for it is he who gives you the ability to produce wealth, and so confirms his covenant, which he swore to your ancestors, as it is today.

Deuteronomy 8:10–18

Now, you would think after all God had brought them through—famines, conquering tribes, enslavement, plagues, and forty years wandering in the desert—the people of Israel would be so overwhelmed with gratitude that they could never forget how far the Lord had brought them. But, like all human beings, their stability and success affected their memories. They forgot to remember all that God had done for them. Even before they reached the Promised Land, they were melting down their gold to create an idol to worship!

So you have to remain authentic to who you are once you're successful—after all, that's how you got to be where you are. Remember what—and who—got you there. You have to remain humble and dependent on the Lord, giving Him the ultimate credit for your many blessings. Yes, you have to work hard and do your part, but He is the One who has anointed you with His favor to live your Full Tank Life. So live in a zone of gratitude and make sure you don't become complacent. In other words, just because you were able to pay it, don't forget the great price of your success!

I remember sacrificing so much time, all my resources, and considerable effort to get to this great quality of life I live in now. But not one day goes by that I don't think about my father collecting beer cans and Coke bottles along the beaches of the Florida where I grew up. Not one day goes by that I don't remember the stench of chicken manure that clung to my clothes after I finished my shift and had to go to school. Not one day goes by that I don't think about what it was like to be told no over and over again. Remembering how high I've climbed makes the summit that much sweeter! And I'm still climbing for higher ground.

Success also comes at a great price for those around you. Your parents, friends, mentors, and other loved ones all contribute at some point or another to your life. For better or worse, you are the product of the people who have influenced the way you think, speak, and act. Honor these people in your Full Tank network by remembering their sacrifices and their belief and support for your dreams.

Full Tank Legacy

No matter how much blessing you experience, always remember who you are, where you came from, and what you did to get there. Like I did, and like most dreamers with a Full Tank, you will have to experience failure and defeat. That is how you learn. When you succeed and reach one major goal, then the pressure will mount to work harder and win again. Expectations, your own as well as others', will rise alongside your success to a height that cannot be reached.

This is why ultimately you must not allow success to define you or change your core identity. Most of the time you will still encounter the same struggles and issues you have battled throughout the process during your journey. Fear will still try to immobilize your motivation and make you a zombie. Depression will come in like a fog and cause you to overthink what matters. But throughout your journey, just remember, God is there with you. He is the One who has preordained your Full Tank Life and all your dreams. In the Bible, God spoke through the prophet Isaiah saying, "So do not fear, for I am with you; do not be dismayed, for I am your God. I will strengthen you and help you; I will uphold you with my righteous right hand" (Isa. 41:10).

At the end of the day, your Full Tank Life is found in Christ alone and all of your wins and losses are His! I believe that our relationship with Christ gives us everything we need. You may not have all that you want to achieve, accomplish, and acquire in your life yet—and in fact, no matter how successful you become, there will always be new mountains to climb. But you already have everything you need: the abundant life Jesus told us he came to bring, the peace that passes understanding, and the joy that cannot be stolen by other people.

Paul writes in the book of Colossians, "For in him all things were created: things in heaven and on earth, visible and invisible, whether thrones or powers or rulers or authorities; all things have been created through him and for him" (1:16). It is all about Him and we want to pass this legacy of faith and gratitude on to others, especially our children…this is our Full Tank Legacy! Your attitude of exuberant gratitude in the pursuit of your dreams will make an eternal difference in the lives of your children and their children.

Pedal to the Metal

Throughout these preceding pages, I've tried to share what I know about living the kind of life I enjoy, the Full Tank Life. Please keep in mind this is not a perfect life or a life of riches and material gain. It's simply a life in which you live out the purpose for which your Creator made you. Simply put, this is the only way to find peace and happiness in this life. You will never be fulfilled chasing after your dreams if you become misguided and start believing their attainment will satisfy you. Nothing you do, acquire, buy, sell, or create will ever be enough by itself. It's all in the process!

You see, the Full Tank Life is one in which you are constantly going at full throttle while also keeping your fuel level steady. You have to make sure you replenish your fuel—through rest, through inspiration, and through time alone with God. When the warning indicator on your dashboard lights up like a Christmas tree, you better pay attention! The joy is in the process of filling up your tank and expending your energy to live out your purpose.

My prayer is that you have learned a few things, laughed a few times, and been blessed by the lessons I humbly offer here. I don't have all the answers or want you to believe my experiences will necessarily be yours. But I do know one thing for sure. If you seek Him and act in faith, God will satisfy the longings of your heart. You are on your way and will be amazed at what God has in store for you. So get your foot off the brake, put the pedal to the metal, and hold on tight—because your Full Tank Life has already started!

Your DESTINY Diary

What obstacles have you already overcome to get to the place where you are now? How can you remember these victories and let them empower you as you face new challenges?

_____

_____

_____

How will you live your life differently now that we're at the end of our journey together in this book? What one message or idea rises above all the others and sticks in your mind? Why is it so important at this present time in your life?

_____

_____

_____

What do you want your Full Tank Legacy to be? Make a list of the mental and emotional qualities and strengths you want to pass down to your future generations. Then make a list of spiritual gifts and life lessons you want your children and your children's children to know. Finally, think about what one action you can take today to begin building this legacy and increasing the inheritance you leave behind on this earth.

_____

_____

Finally, choose a way to celebrate your "graduation" into your new Full Tank Life! It might be having a conversation with a friend over dinner and describing what you've learned from my humble offerings here. Or you could choose to celebrate by taking a step closer to your dreams, such as applying for a promotion or sending your application to finish school. You could even have a Full Tank party and invite everyone to celebrate with you by sharing one of their current dreams and how they're pursuing it. Whatever you choose, make it an expression of your heart, your soul, and your dreams—your Full Tank Life!

ACKNOWLEDGMENTS

My heart is overflowing with gratitude to God for the many talents, gifts, and awesome professionals He used to help me bring my first major book to life. Leading them is my FaithWords/ Hachette Book Group family led by Rolf Zettersten and his amazing team: Joey Paul, Patsy Jones, Laini Brown, Jody Waldrup, Becky Hughes, and Andrea Glickson. I am honored to work with the best literary agents on earth, Shannon Marven and Jan Miller at Dupree/Miller & Associates. Super kudos to my wordsmith collaborator Dudley Delffs for his patient ability to read my mind and help my thoughts transfer to the page smoothly.

Throughout this book I offer motivational nuggets of wisdom for life that I call "BENspirations." While my life has had many ups and downs with many lessons from the school of hard (and soft) knocks, I've also learned that personal experience is not always the best teacher. *Someone else's* experience and takeaway lessons can save others some steps, time, heartache, and money. Consequently, many of my stories and examples come from the sacrifices and accumulated wisdom of my family, my "earthly angels," who continue to share in my Full Tank Life. Not only do they provide wild and wacky material for our weekly reality

TV show on Bravo, *Thicker Than Water: The Tankards*, they've also contributed ample material for this book! In addition to my immediate family and extended family, I would like to thank my two sisters, Patrice and Avalier, who have always been sources of inspiration. And I couldn't do any of this without the love and support of my many friends, fans, partners, and our team at the Destiny Center and Ben Tankard Music.

I also want to thank my mentors and motivators who have pioneered the way, knocked down trees, blazed the trail of motivation, and lit a fire under me for many years. They have each helped me to reach my full potential: my spiritual parents, Rick and Barbara Layton, and my "god-mommy," Dodie Osteen; my friends Joel Osteen, T. D. Jakes, Phil Munsey, Mike Freeman, Creflo Dollar, Jerry Savelle, Jesse Duplantis, Kenneth Copeland, and Bill Winston; and my high-level motivators who continually inspire me to aspire: Steve Harvey, Magic Johnson, Quincy Jones, Tyler Perry, and Oprah Winfrey.

ABOUT THE AUTHOR

Ben Tankard is the founder of gospel jazz music and has sold over four million copies of his award-winning instrumental albums and has written, arranged, and produced for other artists such as Yolanda Adams, Kelly Price, Fred Hammond, Take 6, and Shirley Murdock, with sales of their albums totaling over ten million copies. Reflecting his upbeat, life-enhancing message, Ben's book *Faith It 'Til You Make It* (FaithWorks/BENote, 2002) sold seventy thousand units. In addition to performing, producing, and writing, Ben pastors a dynamic, fast-growing church outside of Nashville, Tennessee, together with his wife, Jewel.

They also star in NBC/Bravo's *Thicker Than Water—The Tankards*, the network's highest-rated freshman reality show with over fourteen million viewers. Depicting their adventures as they lead what Ben calls their "blended, black *Brady Bunch*," the show just wrapped its third hit season with record-setting viewership.

A true renaissance man, Ben also serves as a motivational speaker for the NBA, designs a line of men's clothing, and pilots his own planes. With his faith-filled vision and street-savvy wisdom, Ben loves unlocking the passionate potential in everyone around him. Whether composing, recording, producing, designing, preaching, teaching, speaking, or just laughing and chilling at home, Ben Tankard always runs on a Full Tank.